Into Disaster

Into Disaster

CHRONICLES OF INTELLECTUAL LIFE, 1941

MAURICE BLANCHOT

Translated by Michael Holland

FORDHAM UNIVERSITY PRESS

New York   2014

The essays in this volume were published in French in *Chroniques littéraires du «Journal des débats»: Avril 1941–août 1944*, © Éditions Gallimard, Paris, 2007.

Cet ouvrage publié dans le cadre du programme d'aide à la publication bénéficie du soutien du Ministère des Affaires Etrangères et du Service Culturel de l'Ambassade de France représenté aux Etats-Unis.

This work received support from the French Ministry of Foreign Affairs and the Cultural Services of the French Embassy in the United States through their publishing assistance program.

Cet ouvrage a bénéficié du soutien des Programmes d'aide à la publication de l'Institut Français.

This work, published as part of a program of aid for publication, received support from the Institut Français.

Fordham University Press has no responsibility for the persistence or accuracy of URLs for external or third-party Internet websites referred to in this publication and does not guarantee that any content on such websites is, or will remain, accurate or appropriate.

Fordham University Press also publishes its books in a variety of electronic formats. Some content that appears in print may not be available in electronic books.

Library of Congress Cataloging-in-Publication Data

Blanchot, Maurice.
  [Essays. Selections. English]
  Into Disaster : Chronicles of Intellectual Life, 1941 / Maurice Blanchot ; translated by Michael Holland.—First edition.
    pages   cm
  Includes bibliographical references and index.
  ISBN 978-0-8232-5096-7 (cloth : alk. paper)
  ISBN 978-0-8232-5097-4 (pbk. : alk. paper)
    1. Literature—Philosophy.   2. France—Intellectual life.   I. Holland, Michael, 1950– translator.   II. Title.
PQ2603.L3343A2   2014b
843'.912—dc23

                                                        2013025621

Library of Congress Cataloging-in-Publication Data is available from the publisher.

Printed in the United States of America
16 15 14   5 4 3 2 1
First edition

Contents

Into Disaster

Introduction

MICHAEL HOLLAND

For someone as wedded as Maurice Blanchot was throughout the 1930s to the existence and the idea of France as a nation, defeat by Germany in June 1940, however inevitable it had come to seem, could only signify absolute disaster. And while "disaster" went immediately into general circulation in France as a term that allowed the country to come to terms with what had happened, for Blanchot it acquired an ascendency over all of his thinking from then on, becoming the site of an agonizing collapse of the signifying process itself, a dark beacon lodged in time, recalling and recording the absolute fact that a world, the world, had come to an end.

As if in anticipation of this, the political journalism for which Blanchot was mainly known before the war became entirely anonymous after 1937. With the termination of the heady experiment represented by *L'Insurgé*, a newspaper that appeared weekly from January to October of that year, he withdrew entirely into the day-to-day bread-and-butter activity of a journalist with the daily *Journal des Débats* and the weekly *Aux Écoutes*. We therefore cannot know for sure what part he played in the debates and disputes that leave their trace in the columns of the *Débats* between the start of the war in September 1939 and the establishment of the Vichy government in June 1940. Was he behind the denunciations of censorship in the name of a free press during the course of the hostilities? After June 1940, when, as he wrote to Roger Laporte, every one of his editorials was censored,[1] was he among those who continued to defend press freedom even as the *Débats* were aligning themselves with Vichy and hailing Pétain as the only hope for the future? Is he the author of the first of the articles entitled "After the Disaster," which appeared over four successive days in July, and whose evocation of "the current distress of the French people" and the "immense pain of those who had foreseen the disaster" rings with a pathos that is not unlike what can be heard in the first article in this volume?[2] For the time being, we cannot know any of these things. In his letter to Laporte, Blanchot states that having tried unsuccessfully to persuade the owner of the *Journal des Débats* to close it down, he left the paper, severing all ties with it and returning to Paris where, according to him, his refusal of everything that had happened could most decisively be acted upon.[3]

What is known, however, is that at the height of his personal involvement in radical political journalism in the late 1930s, Blanchot had begun to publish literary articles of extraordinary complexity and penetration in *L'Insurgé*. Three of these "Lectures de *L'Insurgé*" are included in his first volume of literary criticism, *Faux pas*, but to date the rest remain uncollected.[4] A parallel track can thus be seen emerging at this time, one that according to Blanchot represents his true life, that of a "nocturnal" being entirely absorbed by "the movement of writing, its obscure quest," and who differed entirely from the person who signed or did not sign the political journalism that occupied him day by day.[5] This "dichotomy," as he calls it, which can be traced back to the very beginning of his writing career, would now, as disaster loomed, precipitate what Blanchot calls a "conversion" on his part, which allowed him to anticipate and comprehend what he calls the radical changes (*changements bouleversants*) that would very soon occur.[6] The traces of this development are clear to see. Occasional brief reviews in *Aux Écoutes* led in 1938 to an important critical article on Jean-Paul Sartre's first novel, *Nausea*.[7] Then, after the beginning of the war in 1939, Blanchot emerged from anonymity to sign two articles of literary criticism in the *Débats*, one on Nerval, the other on French poetry,[8] and in April 1940 he published an article on Lautréamont in a new journal founded by his friend Thierry Maulnier.[9] But most important of all, the manuscript of his first novel, *Thomas the Obscure*, was with Jean Paulhan in May 1940, and Gallimard would publish it in the autumn of 1941.[10]

During the immediate prewar years Blanchot was also branching out into the wider cultural field. He was a member of the jury of the Prix Réjane in 1938, a prize awarded to actors of stage and screen that was won that year by François Perrier, and in 1939 by Madeleine Robinson. Other members of the jury included Colette and Aurélien Lugné-Poë, the man who staged Jarry's *Ubu roi* in 1896. In June 1940, he was associated with the attempt to take over and relaunch the weekly *Je suis partout* by Thierry Maulnier and others while most of its editors were either under arrest or at the front.[11] This was an abortive project, and Blanchot would pay a price for it: in a review of *Thomas the Obscure* shortly afterwards, he was denounced for his prewar association with *Aux Écoutes* and its owner, "the Jew [Paul] Lévy," and accused of producing a work of "Jewish art."[12] It is noteworthy in this context that when Paul Lévy was obliged to flee France in June 1940, Blanchot defiantly, not to say courageously, allowed his own name to replace Lévy's as director on the title page of *Aux Écoutes*. Lévy returned to France in July, and shortly afterward he was forced by the Vichy authorities to close the paper down.

However, very soon Blanchot would embark on his main cultural venture in these years: membership of Jeune France, an organization founded in September 1940 that sought to work under the aegis of the Vichy government to preserve the cultural heritage and values of France at an entirely nonpolitical level.[13] Blanchot was the literary director of the movement in the occupied zone. Not much is known about this venture in general, or about Blanchot's particular contribution to it.[14] In "For Friendship" he alludes to it briefly and recalls that the actor and director Jean Vilar was also involved.[15] In a recently published letter to his future wife in September 1941, Vilar praises the first novel of "our comrade Blanchot," which he has just read.[16] Less positively, the Vilar archive contains a report written by Blanchot for one of the Jeune France secretariats in July 1941, recommending that Vilar be discouraged from seeking to have his play *Aimer sans savoir qui* (Loving Without Knowing Who) published. Two further indications of where Blanchot was tending at this time are provided by a letter on official Jeune France notepaper to Jean Tardieu, dated September 16, 1941, requesting a poem for an anthology of young poets that he says he is putting together; and another to Francis Ambrière on May 21, in which he speaks of his project for a review and a series of literary collections.[17] Another letter from May 1941 on official Jeune France notepaper was sent to every Paris publisher, requesting the names of "representative" authors from their lists who could be included in an anthology of young poets.[18]

These ventures led nowhere as far as can be seen, and Blanchot eventually resigned from Jeune France, along with a number of others, after what Paul Flamand called the "fifteen frantic months" of Jeune France's existence.[19] Though this was, by Blanchot's account, because the ambiguity of working against Vichy by working for it had become impossible to ignore, it was also because of deep differences within the movement between those like Pierre Schaeffer and Paul Flamand who believed to a greater or lesser extent that art should be at the service of the public, and those like Blanchot and Xavier de Lignac for whom it was a pure ideal from which the national community drew its strength and its identity.[20] Blanchot pursues this debate in a number of the pieces in this volume, in particular "The Theatre and the Public" and "The Writer and the Public." In the meantime, Jean Paulhan had asked him to replace Drieu la Rochelle as the editor of the *Nouvelle Revue française*, in a maneuver designed to prolong its existence and guarantee its independence. This, too, came to naught, since Blanchot eventually refused to take responsibility for a journal in which he himself would not wish to be published, and thereby become the collaborator of a notorious collaborator, as he put it.[21] In December, the Prix Goncourt for *Thomas the Obscure* seemed to be within reach. It went to someone else, but by now Blanchot appeared resigned to withdrawing entirely from the public sphere into that "nocturnal" domain where writing alone could offer a reason to go on living.

In April 1941 he had returned to the *Débats* as the author of a weekly column of literary criticism entitled "Chroniques de la vie intellectuelle" (Chronicles of Intellectual Life), and between then and August 1944 he would publish more than 170 articles. In 1943 a small selection of these texts was published by Gallimard under the title *Faux pas*, and in 2007, Christophe Bident published the remainder with the title *Chroniques littéraires du Journal des Débats.*[22] The articles that appeared in 1941 are published in this volume, with a further three volumes, covering the years 1942, 1943 and 1944, to follow.

It is very clear as we read these articles that Blanchot has now found his feet as a literary critic. The author of the "Lectures de *L'Insurgé*" has come into his own. Though passing allusions to his other activities at the time do occur,[23] he has now placed his reading, his thinking, and his writing entirely at the service of a literary and cultural ideal that, as he loses no opportunity to insist, is absolutely incompatible with what he terms circumstances or events. And if every trace of political polemic has disappeared from his writing, the energy that

inspired his earlier journalism certainly has not. Now, however, it is redirected into sometimes mordant denunciations of
those who allow art to be compromised in any way by association with events or enlisted in the service of a politics of
national revolution, which by implication Blanchot deems a
sham. Already convinced by 1937 that France was no more
than what he called "a nation to come,"[24] after the disaster of
1940 Blanchot sees its future vested entirely in its literature
and culture. This was no tame traditionalism on his part, however, but rather an appeal to what is most radical and adven-
turous in French tradition, which in his eyes is inseparable
from periods of what he terms rupture.[25] The result is an
extraordinarily diverse and colorful series of critical essays, in
which works of lasting quality and significance sit alongside
others that have been justifiably forgotten, and where friendship and loyalty toward those who share Blanchot's ideals play
a decisive role in shaping his attention and his choices.
Though given piquancy by the haughty verve that is always
present in them to some degree, the articles also celebrate in
sometimes ecstatic tones the pure joy and consolation that
literature can bring.[26] Already, a description and a doctrine of
literary art are taking shape, which provide both a defense of
what Blanchot has done in writing *Thomas the Obscure* and
prepare the ground for everything he will go on to write over
almost half a century, as he brings his thought ever closer to
writing the disaster into which history collapsed in 1940.

The question remains: who were Blanchot's readers from
week to week? For whom was he writing? The *Journal des
Débats* was a shadow of what it once was, and its dwindling
readership during the Occupation was hardly likely to respond
well, or even at all, to what Blanchot often forcefully invited
them to consider. Here is a hypothesis: the "Literary Chronicles" were simply a continuation of the intense discussions that
had been going on between Blanchot and Georges Bataille
since their meeting at the end of 1940. What Blanchot says
about contestation in "Vigils of the Mind," not to mention

his reference to the idea that "all authority must be expiated" in "Poetic Works," are just two indications that the thinking that gradually defines and refines itself as these chronicles appear each week is forged in the confrontation between the two diametrically opposed traditions from which each thinker emerged. Somewhere between Symbolism and Surrealism, Paul Valéry and André Breton,[27] a pathway of dialogue is opening up.

As inevitably happens, a number of errors exist in the original articles in the *Débats*. Certain of these are carried over into the versions published in the *Chroniques littéraires*, and I have corrected these. In addition, a number of Blanchot's quotations are either partial or inaccurate, and I have rectified those errors that I am aware of. In general, I have not provided references for quoted text where Blanchot does not. However, where it appeared that it might be helpful, I have done so.

Chronicle of Intellectual Life 1

Bruised and bloodied peoples who cannot express the feelings that beset them will always fall back on reading.[1] And it is to books in particular, even difficult books, that they look for an explanation of what they are. They turn passionately to problems of which they had no inkling. They think they can get the measure of the paltriness of their times that way, and they defend their intellectual honor as best they can. There is more desperate pride than any desire for distraction in such an attitude. Their aim is to abolish time by contemplating human affairs in testimony that will never fade.

There is no doubt that in Paris and its neighboring provinces, a strange thirst for knowledge has led, in less than favorable conditions, to the beginnings of an intellectual revival. Book lovers have begun to appear in countless numbers. Audiences at public lectures have been discerning and loyal. People have discovered within themselves a need to read, to learn, and to know something, even though the only way to impose silence on too noisy a world would have been to pay heed to one or two inner voices, drawn from as close as possible to their original time. The desire to create an ideal spectacle has not been hindered in the slightest by even the most pressing material concerns. On the contrary, outer difficulties and inner insight have had an equal influence on people's souls at the deepest level.

Publishers have thus received a quite inordinate number of requests, given the current circumstances. Their message is always the same: "We are selling technical works as well as novels, dictionaries, and essays in pure thought. If only we could publish as much as we want to. Today's public reads everything." This means that the public is indeed curious about everything, but also that it will accept anything at all. Such confusion is to some extent natural. It is impossible to ask a people that knows for certain only what it rejects, to be very sure also about what it likes. It is very strict about what it does not want, but accommodating when it comes to everything else. Pure as can be when it comes to breaking with certain values and certain mortals, it remains thoroughly tainted by impurities in its frequentations.

What has the response of Paris publishers been to this demand? They have made very laudable and indeed quite remarkable efforts. The difficulties they had to overcome were substantial. They had neither paper nor authors. They had nothing to publish, and they could publish nothing. In short, all they had were readers. But that was enough. They overcame the technical difficulties. In one or two authors they reawakened a desire to write. They even won for themselves a degree of freedom, since as is well known, books are the only intellectual commodity that is not subject to prior inspection. With these means they drew up a program whose implementation has only just begun, but that has already come up with several genuinely interesting works.

In our view some of those works deserve detailed examination, both because of their intrinsic value and because they provide an important record of the period we are living through. But it would seem useful first of all to provide a

brief reminder of what has appeared during the winter and
the spring. Books on topical issues have been neither the most
numerous nor those most frequently read. Events are what
they are. Those who endure them are quite familiar with
them, and prefer silence above all else. However, there have
already been one or two war narratives. A very young writer,
Jean de Baroncelli, has just published a book on the subject
entitled *Twenty-Six Men*, whose qualities are most engaging.[2]
Jacques Benoist-Méchin has published another, with the title
The Harvest of 1940, and it is already famous, while Maurice
Betz has also attracted attention with his *Prisoners' Dialogues*.[3]
These works, like Pierre Mac Orlan's *Chronicle of the End of a
World* or *Private Chronicle of the Year 1940* by Jacques Char-
donne, are too close to our time to escape being caught up in
its enigmas.[4] They contain a darkness into which we simply
peer in vain.

Novels have met with the fate that was no doubt reserved
for them. The passion with which they have been read far
exceeds the rigor with which they were written. They are well-
crafted books and are adequately constructed, but they represent nothing more than a certain fidelity to a mediocre tradition. Excessive praise has been heaped on the first novel by a
young woman named Irène Français, *I Was a Little Girl*,
whose frail charm appealed to people because it was pleasant
and accessible, while also being aimless and chaotic.[5] To be
without artifice is not always the same as to be natural. By
contrast, a first novel from a very young writer, *The Grass Is
Growing in the Meadow* by Raymond Dumay, has qualities to
which we shall certainly return.[6] Although the novel is not
driven to the breaking point that its author seems capable of
reaching, it has a purity that makes it simultaneously both
familiar and dignified. It summons the reader and separates
him ingenuously from himself. It is calm and confident. Mention should also be made of a novel by another young writer,
C.-F. Landry's *Baragne*, which recalls the work of Jean Giono
only through the occasional lapse.[7]

The works that have attracted the most attention are works of intellectual and literary criticism. In the forefront of our minds there must inevitably be the book that Henri Mondor has just devoted to Stéphane Mallarmé, *A Life of Mallarmé*.[8] It is the fruit of extensive labor, and the labor has been successful. Dr. Henri Mondor has brought together a number of admirable texts that cast extraordinary light on the destiny of this prince of the mind. Thanks to his patient search through an immense number of Mallarmé's letters, he has succeeded in extracting words and even confidences from that most silent and sober of writers, who was unsurpassed for intellectual modesty. He has restored a life story to a man whose entire existence lay in his work, which was itself, in all its wonder, as close as possible to being nothing. He has revealed him in his proud simplicity. Today it is a simple yet pleasurable recompense for the mind to be able to contemplate a man who, in total and obscure solitude, was able to hold sway over the world through the pure exercise of an absolute power of expression.

Even after such an important book as this, there are many others that deserve to be examined and brought to the attention: the *Anthology of French Poetry* by Marcel Arland is a selection with commentaries that brings favorably to mind the enduringly successful book by Thierry Maulnier in the same vein.[9] The publication of Montesquieu's *Notebooks*, selected and introduced by Bernard Grasset, marks a date that circumstances will make almost unforgettable.[10] Thanks to the freedom of spirit that it reveals, whose excesses are a sort of challenge to hypocrisy, this book opens up infinite prospects for the mind. Something that is tolerant and yet harsh, affected yet natural fills these fiendish pages where intelligence appears to provoke barbarity through the ease of its power. Finally, in addition to a remarkable biography of Charles Péguy by Daniel Halévy (*Péguy and the Cahiers de la Quinzaine*), we should mention two major translations: *The Birth of Tragedy* by Nietzsche and the *Concluding Unscientific Postscript to the Philosophical Fragments* by Kierkegaard.[11]

This rapid overview takes no account of the true movement of people's minds during these truly strange months. It will be necessary to try and capture that movement in its uncertainties as well as its contradictions. It is a fact that many writers have condemned themselves to silence, less because of the external difficulties they may have encountered than because they have suffered a veritable ordeal of sterility. They have kept silent and they remain silent because they think they have nothing further to say. An arid night has fallen over them. After many years of vain agitation, they have finally heard their own silence. How long will this crisis last? Literature and art are being shaken today by numerous false problems, worrying scruples, and miserable contrition. There is much talk of morality and much talk of wisdom. These grand words, with their concern for tradition and classicism, are generally no more than adornments for mediocrity and impotence. Those who parade about in them are those who are not worthy of them. The others, the truly classical writers, the true writers of tradition, seek extreme wisdom in extreme daring, and desire only to be the masters of their own originality.

—April 16, 1941

The Writers' Silence

It is certainly far from easy to define the doubts that some writers have experienced during the months we have just lived through. Why is it that intellectuals of all kinds have abandoned everything, even mental labor? What thinking or what absence of thinking can have brought them to such an arid ordeal, in which publishing, writing, and reflecting appear like immoral acts that must be harshly forbidden? How did they reach this strange state of repose, which is both an enigma and a self-inflicted purgatory? To look for the causes of such a state of mind at present would be utterly pointless. The reasons that come to mind are all too obvious, and provide an explanation for everything. War followed by defeat, defeat followed by war: nothing can withstand such overwhelming reasons that, on every subject, provide their imperious answer. One can see how, even when it comes to explaining silence, silence has its virtues. Is it not better to put off until later the explanation of a crisis whose true meaning is that we will probably never know it?

Nevertheless, the fact is that a number of books are beginning to appear, that some of them deserve to be read and thought about, and that one cannot read them properly without thinking of the great mass of all those that have not been written and normally would have been, that immense library of absent and abolished books. For someone who has been accustomed to reading, the feeling this inspires is one of the strangest that can currently be experienced. When a work appears—and all in all, a lot of them do—it is impossible not to see something miraculous and exceptional in the fact, so natural would it seem were no one to write again, as if the notion of an author had disappeared in the catastrophe, swept away along with so many other surface appearances. This is the sign of a considerable malaise. All have not experienced it, but all those who have felt its impact know that it is the most remarkable intellectual phenomenon of these times, when books have come to appear as no more than the outer fringe of a laborious silence.

Where does this malaise originate? First and most obviously, in a certain degree of uncertainty concerning the fate of literature and the arts. It is as if several of those who write, not knowing what will be dead tomorrow and what will be alive in the realm of aesthetics, and unable to say which modes of writing will be condemned and which saved, have been overtaken by rather cruel doubts from which only a number of firm prospects could have saved them. Such uncertainty is characteristic of those periods when art receives more enigmas from the world than the world receives from it. At such times, the most extraordinary confusions occur. Crude theorists can be heard to maintain that once there has been a war, everything in the way of daring works and original authors that immediately preceded it must be rejected and trampled underfoot. Denial becomes the supreme critical method. There is repentance for what was once a source of satisfaction. There is shame at former pride. A distant, comfortable past becomes a refuge from risks it is no longer thought desirable to run. But during great upheavals, classicism becomes no more than a dismal refuge, and the minds that come to rest there simply find excuses for their fatigue rather than reasons for any genuine fidelity.

Other theorists, inspired at times by dangerous and alluring ideas, advise both artist and writer not merely to break with the last twenty or thirty years, despite the masterpieces that illustrate them and perhaps because of these, but to devote themselves to a new collective ideal, to enlist in the service of a social order that culture must both express and construct.

This is not an unworthy task. Writers, particularly young writers, can see the dangers of an isolation for which they have so often been criticized. Their minds turn to the public that is formed by their entire nation, and in whose service they are ready to sacrifice a great deal, even their intellectual honor. They reflect on that citizenship without which they are nothing. What must they do to atone for their misdeeds? What mission will be entrusted to them in this immense society of misfortune? To write, be it only masterpieces? What an improper suggestion! They blush at having made it, and despise themselves simply for being themselves, feeling that the persistence and the excellence of their vocation amount to a flaw.

In our view, many artists are experiencing a profound crisis of conscience, and seeking with tragic sincerity by what means other than those of their art they can involve themselves personally in the collective undertaking that they are witnessing. How can they enable the people to participate in a culture that is a priceless treasure? In what way can art be transformed so that it becomes common property? What efforts of discipline are required to enlist thoughts of pure and utter solitude in the service of public order? These problems are not new. The artist has always been drawn to what he alone loves, and only rarely has he succeeded in thinking or painting for mankind as a whole. But it is no less true that whenever times have been difficult, he has suffered doubts about himself that have driven him to reveal his impotence.

Such doubts have never been stronger. We know of various projects being pursued by young men who, in the midst of the general collapse, are seeking to save art by restoring a public to it, or to save artists by turning them into educators of youth. We know too that there are those who have embarked on a critique of excessive individualism, and will now only accept work that is conceived as a paean to the homeland, the earth, and the values of tradition. There are others, finally, who are taking revenge on the gratuitousness of art by bidding the artist to serve, enlist, and compromise himself—not by exercising his talent, which would be perfectly natural, but by adhering to political ideas or principles that he is quite incapable of judging. These appeals come in various guises. They are often accompanied by very serious truths. But they abuse these truths so as to instill in unsteady minds ideas that they cannot control. As a result, it appears to many people that the thinking to be found in great books or great canvases is heretical, and conflicts with the wisdom of these times given over to disaster and turmoil.

The war and our current misfortunes cannot be held entirely responsible for creating a malaise that a few of yesterday's critics already had an inkling of. One of the best artists of his generation, Jean Bazaine recently wrote in the *Nouvelle Revue française*:

> For a few years already we had been witnessing a grand onslaught of mediocrity, bedecked in the fine names for which it has a predilection: tradition or classicism. . . . There was already much talk then of "returns": a return to line, a return not only to subjects but also to "great subjects," and so on and so forth. "French art," as one art weekly put it more or less, "can no longer remain an art of experiment and absence," and that was said at a time when painting, finding itself isolated in a world of decay, had just rediscovered once again the fresh and living wellspring of French art. Who would believe it?[1]

Literature was the target of similar exhortations, and unfortunately, it had begun to obey them. On the pretext of condemning the fine, fortuitous revolt of the post–World War I

writers, minds were lured toward a perfectly empty humanism, offering neither memories nor promise. Young writers,
with a few exceptions, were wary of all inventive originality
and sought merely to express, in pale language, the banal
images of life. They did not know what it was to create. They
had neither a talent nor a taste for it. They had almost lost
sight of the fact that every man who is jealously and power-
fully a person enters a superb world in which his thoughts and
his nightmares, given necessity by virtue of their expression,
acquire the force of an obligatory existence.

   These errors of yesterday, combined today with a variety of
scruples, make up a strange climate in which writing has
become nothing more than a rather suspect activity. Every
author who remains silent gives an icy look to the author who,
obeying what are inevitable reflexes, goes on being productive.
If an author, even more to his disgrace, remains true to himself, and if the work he publishes resembles his previous works,
astonishment turns to scorn, as if it were unbearable that a
writer should naïvely go on living and speaking in the silence
of a spiritual Pompeii. Fortunately, readers are not dead. On
the contrary, they would appear to want to relive, for a few
moments, everything that they have learned over the centuries—the dogmas, the masterpieces, the history—and to
gather together, in the register of their memories, everything
from the past that gave them a reason for being, and everything that can, for the future, give them reason to hope.

                                                    —April 19, 1941

Chronicle of Intellectual Life 2

The narratives of topical interest that have recently been published are far less mediocre than might have been feared. There is a natural quality about them, even a degree of style. They are not without sound judgment, and at least one of them displays literary qualities, while another contains testimony that will probably be read in later years as an authentic reflection of our times and on our times.

Nonetheless, the fact remains that narratives based on current events belong to an inconceivable genre. What do they offer? What are they? They are driven by the events on which they depend and without which they would be nothing. They describe them and they distort them. They lend them what they can, and take from them almost everything. They are neither novels nor histories. What people look for in them is an anomalous amalgam of life, sincerity, and fiction. And in so far as their language is merely an artful patchwork of arbitrary detail and truthful detail, it proves a rather flimsy resource.

Yet such narratives are inevitable. Writers cannot be prevented from believing that they are the masters of the drama they have just experienced. They like to say what they have seen, and they like to think that what they have seen is unique to them. All around them they can sense a general state of expectancy on the part of readers who are ready to read, and that convinces them of the validity of what inspires them. They also have one or two great examples to refer to, such as Goethe, who wrote an admirable war narrative, though admittedly by transforming war into a vast field of experience for himself. But in the end they do not need as many excuses. When someone wants to write, how can they resist weakness of imagination, the urge to create nothing and above all the need to be, inside a book, the person they believe themselves to have already been at the center of a great tragedy?

This sort of autobiography naturally attracts very young writers. It is always the youngest who can remember having been. They are nothing but memory, and what they remember is so much a part of them that in narrating their own story they think they are imagining a new fantasy. And indeed, the first work to be examined is by a writer in the full flush of youth, Jean de Baroncelli. His book tells the story of the war as it was fought by a platoon of twenty-six motorcyclists.[1] These twenty-six men encountered almost every situation that arose during the hostilities. They waited for the war, but were never given the time to experience it. Then they retreated toward Dunkirk. And their retreat drew them into the world of defeat and debacle.

Baroncelli's book has many merits. Its unity of tone and development is sometimes remarkable. These twenty-six men from modest backgrounds seem constantly to be on the outside of what is happening. Even when they suffer because of it and die from it, they are not part of it. They convey it without ever making contact with it. They remain at a distance without appearing to notice this exile. Their succinct dialogues express not the slightest surprise. It is in what is both superficial and precise about their remarks that this attitude can be most clearly perceived. Are they simply out of their element? Are they permanently estranged from their life and their death because they were removed from their true existence too suddenly? This is certainly what Baroncelli implies. But his art is more profound than he is. These twenty-six country people are the heroes of a world they are unaware of. They experience unusual and surprising things without appearing to find them extraordinary, and such natural behavior in the midst of a drama that is far from being so, is the most mysterious and only truly dramatic element in their tragedy.

There can be no doubt that such is the intention behind Baroncelli's book. It gives it real literary value. It could have turned it into a book of considerable worth, had Baroncelli been more conscious of it. His narrative is a curious combination of slowness and movement. Simplified descriptions that are very rapid and very precise follow on from repetitions that occur sporadically. Needless and conventional inner monologues relentlessly drown out the very powerful impression created by an occasional flash of dialogue. Suddenly the author says everything—and thus says nothing—after composing pages of enigmatic reserve and almost abstract concision. What explains this peculiar approach? No doubt a clash of unreconciled influences. In *Twenty-Six Men* there are strong echoes of Péguy, and it is doubtful whether Péguy is a good model for a novelist. It is even far from certain whether that peerless writer should ever be an example for any writer. He is a master and a model of greatness. His work is inaccessible to anyone who seeks to borrow from it an art of his own.

Baroncelli's story is fiction. The author stays close to events, but he shows them to us as if he had invented them freely. Jacques Benoist-Méchin's book *The Harvest of 1940*, on the other hand, presents itself as a historian's account with a documentary value.[2] Benoist-Méchin was a prisoner of war between June 25 and August 15 in a camp situated in the middle of the Beauce region. He tells of everything he experienced and felt, using notes that he made day by day. His book is a very elaborate and detailed diary in which analysis encompasses the facts, attaches itself to them, and clarifies or circumvents them, according to the hopes or griefs of the moment.

No more can be asked of a book such as this than what its author decided to put into it. It is a first-rate piece of testimony, full of strange pathos. The drama it consists of is a drama that cannot be expressed. It exists within the reader as much as in the writer. As he follows step by step, moment after moment, the successive actions of an intelligence grappling with unbelievable events, the observer experiences within himself everything that is harsh, deadly, and impossible about this struggle for the truth. Deep in the murkiest night, what should, what can a man think when his entire life is devoted to honest judgment? What expedients does he resort to, what moments of weakness does he suffer, what fraudulence must he induce in his prostrate mind, and what obligatory self-deception if he is to come to his senses and find his bearings again? This struggle, which is interminable, more exhausting than hunger and more violent than despair, finds in *The Harvest of 1940* a mode of expression that is impossible to ignore. It gives us an inkling of one of the most terrible dramas of these times. It binds us to the conflicting thoughts that have brought turmoil to every mind as if to a succession of furious enigmas. Throughout those days, every man was a prisoner, and his prison was the slumber of instinct and the night of the mind.

Benoist-Méchin tells us himself what the visible subject of his book is: the task of organizing teams who did what they could to save the harvest in a province where it was always very rich. This task allowed him to escape from inside himself, where he was fading away. He put aside the dream that was stifling him and thrust it down beneath the threshold of his will. Each of his duties, every hindrance and every scruple was transformed as a result. He knew the feeling of rediscovering the real in the depths of a nightmare, where reality was initially merely absurdity and falsehood. He gave himself precise obligations. He planned a magnificent escape by attempting to live patiently and methodically for other men and with other men than himself. Comradeship, which seems in his eyes to be primarily ethical in character, became something like a symbol of true deliverance. "Through the other prisoners," he writes, "we reached the true sphere of life, which is one of creation indefinitely pursued and indefinitely extended."

Benoit-Méchin's book contains one or two particularly important pages. When the writer learns that he is soon to be liberated, he experiences a sort of unease. It feels to him that by leaving the camp he is once again going to find himself up against impossible problems. What awaits him is the inextricable mix of the true and the false. The tragedy of judgment is going to begin again. In the grip of confusion, he writes these surprising words: "Am I sure to come out the winner? I'm going to leave the war and enter . . . what?" What can be heard here is the failure of a mind that is vainly seeking a refuge. Beneath the apparent serenity and the appearance of reason and strength, there is a basic anguish that gives Benoist-Méchin's book its moving significance. A yearning for prison, a familiarity with solitude, an unease when confronted with anonymous crowds, a need to live a dutiful life as if one were above the world: these are all products of the anxiety in which everyone has lived and sometimes continues to live: we see in them the methodical, lucid stratagems of a mind that flees from reality into nightmare, then returns from nightmare to reality, in an attempt to delude itself about its true fate.

—May 4, 1941

Two Novels

Raymond Dumay's novel *The Grass Is Growing in the Meadow*
provides its readers with a simple pleasure that it indulges
unquestioningly.[1] How truly pleasurable it is to be able to
describe a good book using adjectives such as "charming,"
"pleasant," or "effortless," which generally apply only to
mediocre ones. These words are suddenly rehabilitated by the
sentiment they express. Reading has become a pleasure, and it
is not clear why. Not to be able to find the reasons for one's
pleasure is itself a reason, and one that embraces all the others.

And yet this little novel contains no secrets. Everything
about it is revealed at first glance. Could this bright, un-
clouded picture, evoking the lives of a few shepherds on the
banks of the Saône, express anything remotely unexpected?
Their amusements, their insignificant deeds, the gentle drift
of their existence are all very far from being novel, and they
adapt themselves to our attention without ever fulfilling our
expectations. After reading this book, we close it with the
thought that we have forgotten everything about it: its facts,
its characters, its words—everything indeed, except for a sense

of purity that is all the stronger for having no cause, or because everything that could explain it has already faded.

One of the great merits of *The Grass Is Growing in the Meadow* certainly lies in its effortlessness, which rises exquisitely above all of the usual complacencies to be found in novels. With his seven or eight shepherds, Dumay could have written a tale or a story, or composed some sort of piece made up of closely linked episodes with a beginning and an end. That method of holding the attention would have been no effort for him. His book contains the outlines of narratives that a minimum of complacency would have allowed him to take advantage of; they are like basic building materials, which a mediocre architect would have transformed into an ordinary dwelling, but which this author, with unhurried artifice, has turned into a sort of landscape through which he wanders ever alert, with a freedom that is at the same time deliberate. He thus quite intentionally deprives himself of the advantages of a story. He takes as his subject one whose characters achieve nothing that can be recounted in a sustained and consistent manner. And, with this constraint, he produces an impression of ease and docile movement that brings to mind a narrative that is constantly being relieved of its consequences.

This novel that is not a story is a rustic novel without a picturesque element. The picturesque, like local color, is made up of ingredients that a writer uses each time he wants to arouse pleasure and interest by means other than those provided by his work. It is the proof that he does not believe in what he is writing. The ornamentation he uses is not to be found in art, but in custom and nature. To describe country people and attribute to them the curious practices that are still widespread in certain provinces is to believe that the book you are writing is of value neither for its inventiveness nor for its form; its existence relies solely on the curiosity that remarkable customs arouse, and on the dishonest appropriation of a certain number of them. It is merely a vain and tiresome surplus.

There is nothing like that in Dumay's book. His shepherds and shepherdesses live as do all young people who spend their days looking after their flocks among trees and by rivers. They have neither past lives nor customs. They are ignorant of everything that goes on. Their youth is nothing but simplicity and freshness. They climb trees, steal fruit, and light fires. Boys and girls play together healthily and sensuously. They fight, talk, and think, and nothing in their language and their thoughts can be linked externally to any sort of rustic oddity. This is something remarkably new. These young peasant folk do not speak the dreadfully conventional language that is usually attributed to them. They are natural without the added artifice that the impossible imitation of a patois provides. They spare us the worst.

All these qualities, though positive and pleasant, do not convey the true quality of the novel itself. It is not highly inventive; its form is straightforward. There is nothing vulgar or mediocre about it, but nor is there anything particularly premeditated, or indicative of any serious effort. Whence then does the pleasure it provides originate? Quite clearly, from the hum of idleness and musing, the murmur of lazy absentmindedness that rises faintly from meadows, woods, and water. All of the scenes we are told about, those unimportant depictions and insignificant conversations, are mingled with scarcely perceptible images that carry a sense of ambiguous purity and life. The carefree delight of each passing day lends its silence to these stories, which scarcely exist. An illusion of indefinite duration casts a transparent film over the bustle and frivolity we are unable to remember. Gradually, we are left with an impression of a world of warmth where time is imbued with the cool of the meadow. We are transported to a sort of pure season where images themselves vanish, and that we savor through an utterly simple, utterly ingenuous, yet secret impression. Whether it be summer or autumn, the moments of the seasons we have known are like the internal links in a story that is not told. And it is in the midst of a nature composed of our idleness and our reverie that the adventures of these fleeting characters unfold.

There are very few things in this little book, but its gaps
and its intervals are arranged with such unerring instinct that
the reader discovers in it a frame that contains a sort of natural
time, formed out of the warmth of plants, the moisture of
water and the haze of sunshine; a type of slumber in which
dreams, like those of hibernating animals, obey the rhythm of
the harvest. *The Grass Is Growing in the Meadow*: the title of
the book also expresses its subject, and the charm to be found
in it comes from the restraint with which that subject is
treated, with neither complacent description nor mythical
ostentation, and with a sort of negligence that sometimes
makes it seem as if the subject has vanished, whereas it survives
intact in that thread of tranquil reverie which winds itself
around effortless or tenuous episodes. That is the sign of a
well-honed talent. Though still very young, Dumay knows the
value of refusal, and his concerns are very different from the
heady delusions with which young novelists are generally
content.

Such foolhardiness is to be found in several of the novels
that appeared almost at the same time as *The Grass Is Growing
in the Meadow*, which are also the work of young novelists.
There is one, however, that does have qualities. Its tone is
vigorous, its development persistent, and it affects a simplicity
that eventually becomes an authentic one. It is very different
from Dumay's book in that it is not a rustic novel that does
not know it and conceals the fact from itself, but on the contrary a novel that displays with a sort of deliberate intent all
the idiosyncrasies and customs of a novel of the land. The
characters are rugged, stubborn peasants. The subject displays
the external symbolism that tradition has made inevitable. A
village is dying because it has no more water; it is reborn in a
place where water has been found; it has to be abandoned,
then rebuilt; the death of the village, the animals that must be
left behind, the despair and the struggle of the people all give
rise to episodes that are far from new.

There is more. The precise form that the writer uses
strangely resembles that of Jean Giono. It does not have the

latter's magnificent extravagance, but it has its mannerisms. For example, here is how a shepherd speaks: "People and towns is just the same. They grows like trees, then they comes down again, they leaves room for others, but remember, there's what goes away, but there's also what comes. . . . So you see: the water went away but the water also came. . . . Where the water is, that's where the village'll be." The entire book is written in this artificial language. You read it as if you are suffering from a delusion, and wonder by what transference of talent the author is able to write so continuously in a language that has hitherto been preeminently the domain of another writer.

However, the main interest of *Baragne* by C.-F. Landry would appear to come from what ought to be its weakness.[2] One is initially irritated by a world and a style that offer so many words that one has already heard; but then one is surprised by the natural quality that emanates from them. A genuine unity and a power that is almost entirely new find expression in what seemed merely like a renewal. In the end, one grants this young author exclusive rights to a power that he uses as if he were the first to discover it. He, too, rises above its misuse. He derives from it something delectable and moving that is under his control. He appropriates it by giving expression to a work that it sustains. Jean Giono, who was initially perceptible behind the achievements of the work, finally dies and is forgotten about. Is it possible to talk of influence here? Is there some deeper exchange at stake? In our view, the influences that result in the creation of a work that is perfectly and completely whole are inconceivable. A sort of switch of authors is what comes to mind, and one says to oneself that there is in this enigma a phenomenon as important as the birth of a totally new and original writer.

—May 22, 1941

France and Contemporary Civilization

A number of publishers have recently brought out books on the subject of France. *Definitions of France, French Studies, France and Contemporary Civilization*, titles like these express concerns that are all too obviously bound up with recent events.[1] Reading them gives the feeling that for many people, France is merely of topical interest. Thinking about them leaves the impression that they are the passing reflection of thoughts composed for an occasion that they do not express.

What is there to say in general about France that is not simply a matter of reproducing a number of well-known pages? The image that each person may form of the country to which he belongs is determined by feelings that are not left unsullied by events. Within the abstract idea of a civilization can be heard the many voices of a personal drama and of a unique dream in which one feels caught up, and from which one is unwilling to be released by thoughts that are of necessity somewhat crude and somewhat vain. One says what is appropriate to the present moment, and sometimes what one says is no more than the echo of one's passion.

An exception must be made, however, for a few pages that Paul Valéry has contributed to a volume in which various highly competent authors study the place occupied by France in the civilization of today, thanks to its philosophers, its scientists and its artists.[2] It contains some quite remarkable studies of mathematics, physics, biology, and medicine in France. In general, these subjects are dealt with seriously. For his part, Paul Valéry has endeavored to define the spiritual and intellectual achievement of France, by examining what its role or its function may have been in the formation of humanity's intellectual heritage.

These thoughts are not all new. Ten years ago, Valéry published a similar study in a book he entitled *Reflections on the World Today.*[3] His outlook on the world is still the same. It is entirely an inner mental vision, which makes its way through the operations and pathways of the intellect as if they formed an abstract landscape whose chasms and contours it traces with no heed for circumstances. He scans their depths, and turns his analyses into an adventure where it possible to get lost, but not to put a foot wrong. He goes infinitely far almost without moving. His intelligence relishes those labors where it can display what is most difficult about it.

It has been pointed out that Paul Valéry regularly publishes his works several times over and in different forms. This custom corresponds to what may be called the secret tendency of his mind. A given text goes through successive editions, as if it needed the varied contact with other texts or the changing shape of its typeface to reveal what it really ought to be. It resembles a solitary lamp, reflected to infinity in a series of mirrors. It shines and shifts in transpositions that spread its brilliance everywhere. Expressed once, his thought is merely what it is. But when repeated, it provides the material for multiple combinations that our admiration eagerly renews. Such a blossoming of different works made out of sometimes identical texts brings to mind a type of literature that would develop according to the rules that govern Maurice Ravel's

Bolero. All of its diversity would lie in the ever more regular
and ever more precise manner of its presentation, beneath
which it would gradually express all the clarity and all of the
enigmas it contained.

The study published today is so close to the one from ten
years ago that it owes nothing to current circumstances. It
sums up the different features of the French mind in a number
of observations that are virtually uncontentious, and are so
general that they inevitably rule out any allusion to events.
"Variety and continuity," writes Paul Valéry, "these are fairly
regular, remarkably rapid oscillations around certain forms of
equilibrium, be they a return to some ideal or a return to
experience, an alternation between the need for novelty and
the need for the authority of tradition: those seem to me to be
the most obvious and consistent features of what France has
provided, taken as a whole."[4] This variety and this harmony,
whose finest flower is a culture that is both very rich and very
individual, the perfect expression of the French mind and an
image of the universal spirit, cannot be divorced from the variety of soils, men, and languages that have contributed to the
creation of the French people. It is quite true that our country
has sometimes resembled a tree that has undergone many
grafts, the quality and flavor of whose fruits are the result of a
fortunate blend of the most diverse saps and juices, all com-
bining to form a single indivisible entity. The great diversity
of our ambitions comes from the wide diversity of bloods and
the very varied climates that instead of dividing us into a set
of unstable, composite products have made France into the
most distinctive actor on the European stage, the creator of a
characteristic culture and mindset. As Paul Valéry puts it, the
chemical formula corresponding to the French people is one
of the most complex ever, yet the human system it represents
is marvelously unified.

There is nothing in these remarks to conflict with the views
of all those writers who have written about France over the
centuries. They are thoughts that form part of our common

heritage. More important is the role that Valéry attributes to a concern for form in the formation of our culture. France is known to have a predilection for language. Literature for her is merely a particularly rigorous way of cultivating the properties of that language. Culture shows itself through style, and style results from a special sensitivity to words and their arrangement. This concern is undeniably one of the characteristics of the French spirit. Artists and writers have always been struck by it, whether it be Richard Wagner, who memorably declared, "I have to grant the French an admirable talent for giving precise and elegant form to art and life,"[5] or Joseph de Maistre, who wrote rather grandly, "Perhaps things are only fully understood . . . when the French have explained them."[6] Either as a mark of the highest praise or with the secret intention of discrediting her, every single person has emphasized the supremacy that France has succeeded in winning for herself by means of an imperious language, which has made her capable of more influence than she could ever have exerted without the power and talent of expression.

A characteristic such as this, which Valéry emphasizes all the more zealously for having always very consciously made both the methods and nature of his art depend upon it, should not be interpreted carelessly. It is all too easy to understand *form* as the verbal envelope of a thought, and to contrast it with *content*, in keeping with the principles of traditional analysis; in this case, considerations of pure form and the talent that can be devoted to it also signify a degree of indifference towards ideas and values. If such an interpretation holds true for daily life, where words and thoughts refer to the actions they must eventually result in, it has no meaning in the world of culture. Here it is clearly apparent, as Valéry says in another essay, that what is termed content is merely impure form, composed of disorderly words and vaguely apprehended sentences. When someone thinks of the content of a work he inevitably thinks of a few words, a few figures, a few turns of phrase for which he provides a vague equivalent, before they are exchanged for the more precise and more real discourse that will be the form in the strict sense. In that sense, to write well is to go from a fragment of language to a language that is complete, where precisely what remains unexpressed is felt and perceived more authentically than it was inside the murk of inner events; and in the same way, to be master of the content is to be master of the future form without which that content would be examined or invoked to no avail.

It goes without saying that these remarks would need to be completed by other infinitely more important ones, whose purpose would be to show how form overflows language and expression. The creation of a form is the supreme artistic task, and such creation, which is comparable for the artist to the creation of a world, leads him to a pitch of demand where the words, the pace of a sentence, the choice of a figure, the very nature of the characters and the story in the case of a work of fiction, in short everything must depend on a secret scheme, an inner organization, a network of necessity that subjects all of the forces of invention to itself. It is a matter of discovering a law that will give the true artist access to the mystery of things, by allowing him to represent it through the mystery of words. Out of this law there emerges a universe where men obey words, their relations, their outer beauty, and their apparent simplicity, in such a way that both the explanation of human destiny and the dignity of language are elevated to the highest level. And that law itself is merely consciousness of a certain form, which is to say of a poetic order.

There is no doubt that it is in the search for that form that French literature and the French mind have excelled. To be convinced of this one has only to think of the strangely successful way in which French poetry, from Maurice Scève to Paul Eluard, has been able to bring together the wish to dominate the universe of words and the wish to use that very domination to subject the real universe to itself. There can truly be few literatures in which a poet, without a hint of delirium, simply by means of the rigorous study of forms, could have been capable of conceiving the project for a book that would truly be the equivalent of the absolute. That ambition, the torment and the glory of Stéphane Mallarmé, purges French literature of much of the mediocrity that the vanity of writers has brought to it. When one thinks of the author of *A Throw of the Dice*, one says to oneself that the literary pride that is so characteristic of our spirit is a phenomenon of which we should not be ashamed, since there are in our literature a few texts that have aspired with some degree of success to take the place of universal creation.

—May 26–27, 1941

The Art of Montesquieu

We cannot be too grateful to Bernard Grasset. His efforts at familiarizing us with a great classical work that while not unknown was read by almost no one, have been remarkable. He has lavished attention on it. He has placed at its disposal all the inventiveness of an incomparable art of presentation. He has treated it with as much fervor and as much care as he would have done were it a book by a young unknown who deserved to be discovered. Many simple people will have him to thank for revealing the name Montesquieu to them, and praise like that should make him justifiably proud.

The history of these manuscripts, which were not unpublished but had been badly published, is now well known. Bernard Grasset tells how a work on which all men of letters should have had their eyes fixed remained in the shadows and eluded scholarly attention. Having neglected it, the Montesquieu family's sole concern was to conceal it. Having initially avoided publishing it, they brought out an edition that was prevented from becoming widely available, restricting the rare pleasure of reading it to a few bibliophiles. Part of it was known, because the Bibliothèque Nationale held the first volume, but the work as a whole had few readers. Its magnificent publication by Bernard Grasset has thus rescued from obscurity a book with which no one was familiar any longer.

It is clearly remarkable that, a little more than two centuries after they were written, these thoughts should bring new favor to a great writer; but it is even more extraordinary that this writer should precisely be Montesquieu, and that this favor should be bestowed on him at a time when it is no less necessary to us than it is to him. The timely nature of this glory implies a sort of deep-laid plan that cannot simply be attributed to the shrewdness of one man. It is as if the destiny of French literature had held the reputation of this often unbelievably daring book in suspense, in order to keep it in reserve for our era, which is so hostile to all boldness of thought. The name Montesquieu, that perfect symbol of the free spirit, was destined to be repeated as if it were the name of a young author in the very year when young authors have shown very little intellectual ease. And given that we are unable to appreciate any critical rigor in the works that are ours today, we were fated to admire it in a work that, after two centuries, still strikes us as totally new.

Montesquieu's Notebooks as Grasset has compiled them, using a variety of texts on man, morals, literature, politics and history, certainly do offer a new perspective on the workings of a mind that was prepared to sacrifice everything, even its own works, to preserving its freedom of attention.[1] We find ourselves in the presence of an intelligence that sees everything as a pretext for ensuring its independence. It is curious about an infinite number of things, for this curiosity allows it to enjoy a liberty that is almost a libertinage. It turns up everywhere it can be contradicted, without that contradiction ever shaking its resolve. It considers everything that is apparently natural, whether laws, religions, or customs, which is to say everything that could tempt it into granting its tacit consent, and transforms it into a model of peculiarity and oddity. From being a prisoner of the familiarity that comes from use, judgment becomes free again when faced with the absurd. It is liberated through surprise.

There is a case for saying that Montesquieu's intelligence was superior to some extent thanks to his genius for provoking astonishment. Everything he invented tended to distance people from what they thought they knew best, by revealing to them a capacity for being astonished by it. In order to surprise them, it pretended to give itself a surprise of its own. It feigned ingenuousness in response to an entirely artificial civilization, so that this ingenuousness should sow the seeds of unease and give cause for reflection. It pretended to be ignorant so that this ignorance, like an implacable shrewdness, might call everything into question, and above all what appeared to go unnoticed. It stripped time of its familiar outer appearance and gave it one that was unforeseen; and it did so not by renewing knowledge, but by banishing that knowledge and replacing it with astonishment. "How is it possible to be a Persian?" That is the question posed by surprise itself at the moment when it turns toward others before being reflected back on itself.

What is especially remarkable and probably most typical of Montesquieu is the fact that this curiosity, this love of surprise, never affected the self-assurance or the serenity of his judgment. Bernard Grasset draws our attention insistently to all those thoughts where Montesquieu describes to us his capacity for happiness. But this contentment would have been merely a character trait of no importance, had it not been accompanied by an insatiable urge to enquire into things that was capable of moving and disturbing the most self-confident of minds. In fact, it is hard to know what to admire more: the ingenuity with which he shakes up convention, unsettles custom, and envelops people in surprise and astonishment; the tranquil strength with which he confronts the uncertainties of which he is the author; or the absence of any feeling of anxiety as he advances above the abyss he has created for himself, and into which he will not allow himself to fall.

This is the way that intelligence preserves from attack the formal liberty to which it lays claim. There is in Montesquieu a joy of the mind that forbids him from considering his own ways of proceeding as frightening, however perilous they may be. Where he ought to feel threatened by the vigor with which he criticizes his own personal order, he merely delights in the intelligence that allows that critique, and rediscovers in the rigor with which he pursues it the certainty of which he is deprived. By its resolve, intelligence provides him with a stable order at the very moment when it deprives him of it. And the pleasure of expressing it well brings with it a security and a delight that dispel once and for all any hint of anxiety.

This love of surprise, combined with an intellectual serenity that is surprised by nothing, found the form it called for in a language of studied liveliness. Montesquieu's art is quite similar in its use of abstraction to Jean Giraudoux's in the way it handles images. Each of them begins with either a fairly natural observation or an almost banal metaphor, and through an uninterrupted sequence of remarks or images, draws from it an irresistible series of increasingly paradoxical assertions or impressions until, in a concluding sentence, its pursuit having left behind a dazzling wake across the entire surface of the text, the moral or poetic truth explodes in a total yet totally justified antithesis. Very often this inner dialectic is omitted in Montesquieu. We know only the starting point and the conclusion, which are linked together in a refractory alliance that is the more solid, the more surprising it is. The ultimate goal of this style is not just to surprise us but also to capture us through surprise, and to convince us precisely to the extent that we find ourselves placed at a distance. Before we have discovered anything about it, we are touched by the harmony of dissonance.

The *Notebooks* provide only a few remarks about how aware Montesquieu was of this procedure in which he excelled. They are enough to reveal that he slowly premeditated all those bizarre harmonies and disconcerting coincidences. That freest of free spirits had no qualms about unburdening himself of his secrets. "To write well," he notes, for example, "you should skip the intermediary stage of an idea, just enough so as not to be dull, but not so much that you cannot be understood." Similarly, he says a good deal when he writes, "The King of Prussia asked why it was that he did not like women:—You would be annoyed if I told you.—No, he said.—Sire, it is because you do not like men. That is an excellent reply because it contradicts the one you would expect." This, then, is the way to write fine things for Montesquieu: You must persuade the mind to expect a certain direction of argument, and finally, from an unforeseen angle, draw from it the opposite of what it was expecting, so forcing it to be the disconcerted author of its own contradiction, and bringing together in it, with its consent, what it thought it had put asunder once and for all. To say, "Only those with a mind can appear stupid" as he does at the end of one his thoughts is initially nothing more than an amusing joke; but to say it at the conclusion of a development that makes the statement not just probable but certain, is to make a clash of words bring forth a light that provides a dazzling surprise.

To reflect on the role that Montesquieu gives to astonishment is to understand all of the pleasure that these *Notebooks* provide, and also some of the disappointments they hold in store. For the preconditions of surprise change as customs change. Ignorance today is not what it was in 1750; there is less knowledge, or else it is of a different sort. There are contradictions that are no longer apparent, and contradictory relations that are no longer inevitable. Consequently, no longer finding in these maxims all of the surprises they once concealed, we decide to examine them further, and instead of appreciating what is apparent in them, we admire the actions and the stratagems of a mind that is wonderfully skilled at contriving and undoing, with surprising speed, the twists and turns of a sentence. We never tire of admiring the wealth of abstract combinations and pure actions. And as we follow them, we experience a little of the exquisite pleasure that this great mind took in creating them. One of those already familiar texts that the *Notebooks* publish again shows us everything that can be expected of art of such determination, when it is grounded in sentiment that does not weaken it. "I had come up with a plan," writes Montesquieu at the beginning of a projected companion volume to *The Spirit of Laws*, "to give more scope and more depth to some parts of that work; I have become incapable of doing this. My reading has weakened my eyes, and it seems to me that the light they still can see is merely the dawning of the day when they will close forever. I have almost reached the moment when I must begin and end, the moment that reveals and conceals everything, the moment mixed with bitterness and joy, the moment when I shall lose even my weaknesses themselves. Why should I still bother about a few frivolous scribblings? I seek immortality, and it is within me."[2]

So speaks the sensibility that informs a totally intellectual art. It is touching to observe the precision of this emotion, which is like the echo of the ultimate silence that it foretells.

—June 2–3, 1941

The Search for Tradition

The books that have appeared over the last few months have fortunately not paid much heed to events. We have drawn attention here to one or two works that have been inspired by current circumstances, and that are not without their merits. Otherwise there have been very few whose sole justification lay in their topicality. Among all the works, be they novels, poems, or essays, that must, almost of necessity, remain oblivious of external hopes and fears—virtually none has attempted to adapt to the needs of the present. The desire to please the historian, which is a great temptation, has so far affected only the authors of articles and pamphlets.

Nevertheless, it is impossible to ignore the preoccupations of a number of critics, who express their passion not only through opinions drawn from everyday convention, but also through hasty and superficial theories that are the vacuous mirrors of their own disarray. They are unstinting with their warnings and advice. With the fine zeal that comes of living for the moment, they aim to reform genres, impose subjects, and mold the whole of intellectual life according to what their current preferences dictate. What do they want? Must writers and artists become the illustrators of what just happens to be the theory of the day? These are the precepts of fragile minds, eager to imitate rather than be.

These directives are perfectly natural but in reality quite unimportant. In a recent article, a young writer named Francis Ambrière, who is currently a prisoner of war and who, in the camp where he is being held, manages to publish a remarkable newspaper every month, quotes the following lines, sent to him by a friend in Paris: "Yes, publishers are becoming uneasy and establishing their own censorship, but there are few writers who manage to avoid being prophetic and peremptory. Why must the true values of our generation be vilified?" These remarks are of course pertinent, but as Francis Ambrière says, after every social upheaval, shortsighted saviors are a dime a dozen, and their loud professions of faith reveal merely their own vain desire to be saved. When all is said and done, it is easy not to hear them. "We prisoners," Francis Ambrière says in his conclusion, "are protected by our isolation from this discordant chorus, which reaches us only as a muffled echo. When we return, we must not add our own noise to it, but rather impose our silence on it."

Forming the preface to a novel by Robert Francis, a number of remarks in a similar spirit offer a defense of the writer's right to continue with his work as if nothing had happened. "The intellectual life of a nation such as France," he writes, "cannot fall into line, to order, with some moral code hastily derived from recent events. I might add that I do not even find that desirable, for such an operation would probably lead to the worst possible misunderstanding and the worst possible error, by merely allowing a few works and a few people, hastily repainted in the colors of the day, to deceive the public yet again." Robert Francis goes on to recall the story of Saint Aloysius Gonzaga, which Péguy relished. "What would you do," Aloysius Gonzaga was asked while still only a child, "if you were told you were going to die in a few moments?"

"Well," said the child, "I'd go on playing with my ball." Robert Francis claims the right for writers to resume their labors at the point where they were interrupted by the war. And he himself has set an example by publishing a novel entitled *Imaginary Memories*, which contains all of the brilliant qualities that made his previous works so pleasing, and which have scarcely diminished with use.[1]

What all these reactions show is that the frenzied nature of current circumstances has had little effect on people's minds. Minds defend themselves by dreaming, and that provides them with all the solitude they require. Yet, insofar as one or two people feel the need to guard against it, we must acknowledge that a peril does indeed exist. It is after all astonishing that Robert Francis should have felt it necessary to provide his far from topical novel with this topical preface, and to give an explanation for the perfectly natural continuity of his dreams. Is it because he caught himself thinking like the sort of reader or critic who would rebuke him for being true to himself, and writing books too similar to those of yesterday? Did he examine himself anxiously because his talent had not been affected by the war? He quotes the following words by Jean Vignaud: "I expect novelists now to abandon rules worthy of overgrown children that were fashionable before the war, and which moreover bore witness to our exhaustion and our decadence, and at long last to paint the great social frescoes of our rebirth."[2] Such observations recall the hopes of the first Bolshevik leaders when they called on authors to write totally new masterpieces in honor of their regime. Clearly, nothing is more naïve; but nothing comes more naturally to the mind of the reformer.

Other signs reveal the growing impairment that events are inflicting on the critical mind. A few days ago, twenty young painters put on a collective exhibition of their most recent work in a Paris gallery and gave it the title "Painters in the French Tradition." Since most of them show signs of that spirit of invention whose demands have been reflected in French painting since the nineteenth century, they quite rightly made a point of appealing to tradition, while emphasizing that fidelity to tradition does not consist in being faithful to certain forms but is a search for the genuine creativity without which nothing can be transmitted and nothing endures.

Despite the unremarkable nature of these observations, the critics responded to them with extraordinary surprise and confusion. They appeared to find themselves incapable of understanding that artists whose aim is to blaze new trails in regions already identified by Picasso, Matisse, or Bonnard could possibly lay claim to a lineage lying within the history of French art. In their view, these people could call themselves avant-garde painters, or the painters of tomorrow, but not artists with a concern for tradition. What they held against them was thus not so much their desire to recreate works by giving themselves new rules, as their ambition to remain, by means of these works, in conformity with the great models of the past.

Such thinking reveals a strange fatigue of the mind. When one observes these critics who endlessly talk of a return to classicism reserving their praise for the most mediocre and insipid efforts, for the products of unstudied imitation, one wonders what weakness of imagination, what banality of form is to be found, according to them, in the works from the great creative periods, which were all great periods of rupture. What on earth do these classics that they admire and wish to imitate represent for their minds? And what can this imitation be, if they conceive of it as a sterile observance, as the preservation of a form whose justification has vanished? In fact, it is crystal-clear that classical works only found themselves in harmony with an almost interminable timespan because they appeared to come from somewhere above and beyond their time, tearing through it and burning it up with an extreme concentration that embraced within itself the past, the present, and the future.

To this, the reply from some quarters is that there are many weaknesses in these novice works, and even an element of imitation in their experiments. That is quite possible, and also perfectly natural. How can we expect serene and definitive perfection from artists who set themselves formidably difficult problems, in an effort that requires them to forgo all the facilities of realism? In addition to the fact that they are not all equally talented, and that some of them, incapable of creating forms themselves, are content to borrow those that recent models place at their disposal, it goes without saying that their endeavors lay them open to failures, errors, and even unconscious repetitions of every sort. The ambition they confront threatens to destroy them at every instant. They are to some extent belittled by the difficulty of their task. They appear less than they are because they would need to be more than themselves.

These dangers are undeniable, but it is all the more necessary to seek them out if one is to learn how to master them. What counts is a certain attitude of mind in the face of art, an attitude that is not inspired in any way by a taste for novelty as is sometimes thought, but rather by an inner demand and by the necessity of creating a world that will give expression to everything that one is capable of being. This method is made up entirely of invention and effort. It claims to imitate only by creating. It does not simply use the successes of the past; it asks them for the secret of success, by showing itself to be as capable as they were of daring, rigor, and pride. After acknowledging its failures, it says without risk of contradiction: "My experiments may well count for next to nothing alongside the works of the great masters, but there is no way that the superiority of their style over mine can permit me to abandon the search for a style of my own." And it adds: "What I have inherited from tradition, over and above the knowledge it provides, is precisely the need for a style, that is to say the idea of a form in which rules, appropriately chosen, preserve the values which I express from the effects of time."

There is no doubt that this spirit of creative adventure has only ever been lacking during periods of decadence. It is to it that we owe all the riches and vitality of the period known as the *après-guerre*, which is unjustly maligned by certain young critics. Today it would be a very serious matter if, in the name of wisdom and a return to humanism, circumstances were used as a reason for recommending idleness as a sort of vocation and for discrediting creation in favor of imitation in literary and artistic works. It may well be that the absurd and the fantastic, arbitrariness and vague confusion, will threaten all artistic experiment for a while, turning it into a sort of subject for scandal. But there can be no doubt that periods that do not want to take this risk, and prefer to live as parasites on the great centuries of creation, are doomed to suffer a spiritual degradation that makes them unworthy of the models they have adopted. They wish to inherit the past yet keep it in the past, and are thus incapable of passing it on. They are not even capable of admiring it.

—June 16–17, 1941

The Novel and Poetry

The latest novel by Audiberti, *Urujac*, will appear curious, very fine but unintelligible to some of his readers.[1] Though unable to put it down, they will finish it without understanding it. From page to page they will be carried along on a flood of words that will appear to them to be both bathed in light and impenetrable. At various moments they will have the impression that they are in the hands of an author whose only law is chance. At others, they will feel certain that a meticulous network of precautions and an extremely well ordered system of episodes is enclosing them and leading them on. They will constantly find themselves in the situation of the sleeper who dreams he is falling and does not know where he will fall, or even whether he is falling at all. And when they reach the end, they will leave it behind with no awareness of the key with which it provides them.

Audiberti is one of the most important writers of a generation whose youth is still not entirely behind it. In reality, the title of writer is not totally suitable in his case because of the conventional character it may well lend his talent. It is tempting to imagine that the power he has at his disposal could well be expressed through mysterious activities that are quite foreign to common custom. His true condition makes him an author and a man capable of enhancing what he touches through the resounding display of what he is. Alongside *Urujac* he has just brought out a collection of poems that display a surprising mix of grandeur and poetic guile. The most obscure and punctilious beauties combine with an outpouring of brilliant prankery. Both their precision and their facility offer the image of a style that sometimes triumphs over the forces of expansion, and sometimes yields to them in curious fashion.

Reading *Urujac* offers further proof of these differing qualities. It is easy to imagine a reader who, having entered this forest of words, would go from one end of it to the other without noticing at any point what thread the novel is allowing him to follow as it progresses. All he would see would be immensity, force fields, and nights chock-full of shadow and confusion. Then, having reached the end of this blind journey in which dense words arranged in magnificent periods provide the only episodes, he would retrace his steps through the maze he has just traversed, when suddenly he would discover the trace of a perfectly distinct path, which would reveal to him with almost disturbing clarity the entire development of the story, until this story, by its peculiarity, appeared to him like the shadow of some moral or some symbol, linked to events that are immediately contemporary. There are thus three possible ways of reading such a novel. The first way entails admiring only the sequence of words, the development of images, the caprice of a verbal inventiveness whose richness is similar to that of dream. The second way ignores the development of this superb prose, which becomes its own spectacle and constructs an authentic fiction out of its own twists and turns: What matters now is to bring the story to light and reveal the anecdote that it seemed initially possible to forgo. Finally, this story itself appears to be mysteriously guided by a symbolic intention that, however discreet it may be, remains the true guide to the whole book and gives it its ultimate justification. There are thus three works linked together here, and the way they overlay each other both attracts and repels the eye in a delightful to and fro. The difficulty one has in reading finally gives rise to an entertainment in which fatigue has its part to play.

Urujac is a strange region near Toulouse where one of the heroes of the book, a dentist, who is moreover wholeheartedly inclined to see the world as a gigantic jaw full of rotten teeth, thinks he has encountered a primitive human, or rather an example of early man, the harbinger of the races of today, man at his beginning. In a region where living in close proximity to prehistoric caves has accustomed people to thinking about the first humans, this discovery has a resonance that imbues it with a powerful necessity. It would seem that in this magic realm, man at his origins, original man, can show himself without needing to be protected against the absurdity of his appearance. What is he precisely? A tramp who makes a mysterious living by poaching, keeps live trout concealed about his person, is surrounded by his own rarefied element and is sometimes the source of rather strange-sounding laughter. Having got close to him one day, the dentist notices what amounts to incontrovertible proof: The incisors of the primitive being are like bull's teeth. Such is the man to be found in *Urujac*. The book's entire story is provided by the tale of an outlandish expedition, which sets out to find this constantly elusive man who nevertheless gives the impression that he is everywhere. The members of the small group who take part in the hunt, believing they are in pursuit of the shadowy object of their desires, enter an underground passageway that transforms them for a few moments into cavemen. They are eventually rescued from this mishap, but their dream leaves them with the sense that they have been in contact with a magical power that gives them confidence in themselves and favors the success of their undertakings. However, they feel the urge to return to these caves, where they hope to probe deeper into the secrets of their destiny. But unfortunately, they prove incapable of understanding what primitive man is or where he is, and what emerges for the last time from this underground world is a wretched column of men, riven by rancor and mortification.

It is naturally no surprise that Audiberti's story never once displays the precise lineaments of a continuous form. This is not a matter of degrees of verisimilitude, of reality or of fiction. From episode to episode, the story itself changes genre and changes sense. Sometimes it appears as a sort of tall story, enhanced by Surrealist trickery. At others it expresses with agonizing seriousness the drama of human beings grappling with rudimentary feelings. The man from *Urujac* is present wherever men are aware of what calls to them from deep within their species. His laughter can be heard across the night, when the night is exposed as something made out of organs, and filled with physical expectancy. He shows himself amid a blur of faces like a flash of ignorance, like the all-powerful revelation of what cannot be understood. He is a specific individual and the image that everyone can see in their mirror. His message ultimately needs to be completed; he is the oracle who cannot be heard unless we talk louder than he does, drowning his voice with a voice that overpowers it and in doing so makes it resound.

That is undoubtedly one aspect of the narrative. But there is another, and it is much less easy to pin down. This story, which is sometimes told by the author in the first person and sometimes by its protagonist, turns out to coincide with contemporary events. It is during the debacle that the narrator meets the dentist whose discovery has set in motion this surprising adventure, and it is during those same days that, having become acquainted, thanks to the manuscript that recounts them, with all the episodes of the great chase, he accompanies the investigators when they return to the cave and witnesses the fiasco of their ultimate downfall. It goes

without saying that the totally modern setting and the conver-
gence of two different series of episodes are not the product
of arbitrary invention. However well Audiberti has discreetly
blurred the historical circumstances surrounding these days,
however much he has kept his story almost outside of time, it
is impossible not to feel how much he has sought to make the
development and the meaning of his story depend on hidden
thoughts that relate to our times. He writes the following
about the manuscript in which the story of the dentist's confrontation with the man of *Urujac* is recounted: "It truly
seemed to me as if I had lived these pages, these adventures.
. . . I sensed that it would fall to me to bring them to a
conclusion, to provide them with a moral, with an end." And
this is indeed what he seems to have wanted to do in a few
enigmatic lines at the close of his book. Here there is a sudden
allusion to soldiers in retreat; but no sooner has he begun to
evoke them than he falls silent. It is as if the author has whis-
pered a message to them that the reader did not need to know
about. He has placed in their possession mysterious, perfect
words about which all further thought must cease.

A writer is of course always free to choose a soul for the
work he wishes to create, and a reader can merely express vain
regret at finding in a work the echo of something that appears
foreign or extraneous to it. What seems to diminish the value
of *Urujac*, however, is the fact that the deeply obscure symbol
to which it submits seems in the end to be the author's personal creation, the mark of an abstract idea whose influence
the story passively endures. To notice this conclusion is to
realize that it was there all the time, driving the various twists
and turns of the book like a moral, arbitrarily directing the
episodes, bringing them to a head and resolving them from
without in accordance with its own needs and requirements.
Who knows what the reader may think when such a doubt
takes hold of his mind. He may conclude that the author,
having set out with a very clear idea of the exemplary meaning
he wished to give his book, has intentionally made the idea

obscure, thrusting it into the depths of his text so that its meaning should not have the appearance of a lesson; he may reflect that the author has made this lesson all the more obscure for having been perfectly clear to him, and may wonder if he is not the victim of maneuvers whose contrived nature appears to derive more from a politics of the mind than from any mythic necessity. Major doubts of this sort leave him feeling deeply uneasy.

Hence, if Audiberti can be reproached for anything in *Urujac*, it is for having been too cunning an architect of his work, by constructing around what is perhaps merely an episodic symbol the form of a book whose entire strength depends on the surprising illuminations of language. Instead of losing ourselves in a search for naively contrived intentions, we thus come back with the greatest and purest pleasure to the life of images, to the brilliancy that an extraordinary explosion of words scatters throughout the entire book. Some of its pages possess inimitable power and subtlety. The account of the frenzy that, deep inside the caves, transforms pathetic little modern men into primitives cast far outside of time is a triumph of inspired virtuosity. The rigid, immutable words of our language suddenly become capable of extraordinary metamorphoses. They break their chains without losing their value; they form unexpected figures before which they then recoil in fright; they compose themselves and destroy themselves in a turmoil that the author directs as if it were a vague game that he never ceases to control, even when his words seem to be carried away by their own violence.

An attentive reading of these pages reveals the contradictory qualities that gave rise to them. We see a writer whose verbal genius lies entirely in its own passion, a highly conscious author who rejects all the facilities of improvisation. We gain the sense of a poet who obeys words, and of another who disciplines them to such an extent that he recreates them. Alongside the man who acknowledges no other rule but his own talent, there is a man who puts it through all manner of difficulties and trials. What an admirably monstrous combination, what a delightfully scandalous mix. How is it tolerable to find that the same author has, like Janus, a double face: one turned toward Victor Hugo, the other toward Mallarmé?

—July 7–8, 1941

Culture and Civilization

Everyone knows the famous words that Paul Valéry attributed to civilizations in 1919: "We, we civilizations now know that we are mortal. We had long heard tell of whole worlds that had vanished, of empires sunk without trace with all their men and all their machines."[1] Exactly a century earlier, in 1819, following another universal storm, a rather modest writer named Ballanche expressed the same anguished doubt:

> You constantly say, "What will become of the human race?" I see civilization sinking deeper every day into an abyss where all I perceive is widespread wreckage. . . . You also say: "History tells me that ordered societies have perished, that empires have ceased to exist, that deadly eclipses have cast a shadow for several centuries over humanity." And I can see today analogies that make me tremble.[2]

This is almost the same language. In any case it amounts to the same thinking. The word "civilization" is linked to the word "death." Through the danger to which they expose them, great historic upheavals restore the prestige of both the works that they threaten and the names that are associated with them.

Reasoning of this sort is no doubt behind the widespread use of the word "civilization" and the word "culture" that is made today by political commentators, writers, and people of all sorts. Rarely has there been such talk of culture, cultural education, or the values of civilization. Serious studies as well as superficial publications complacently employ this vague and splendid terminology. Everything that is specious and unreal about a sonorous term is put to use by minds that, driven by anguish, want to talk about what they love the most yet are at the same time content to talk about it irresponsibly. "Culture" and "civilization" are like passwords indicating paths that lead nowhere, or like "Open sesames" intoned before a roadblock.

Repeated recourse to these terms is no guarantee of their meaning. If the use that is being made of them remains as general and unthinking as it is for very much longer, there is a risk that the best minds will go to the other extreme and distance themselves from them, seeing them as nothing but grand words that have been definitively destroyed by custom and habit. The word "culture" in particular is at risk of being disqualified by the barbaric adjective "cultural." "Civilization" is less debased. But when it comes to finding out how the meanings of these nouns relate to each other, what enigmas they conceal or what value the way language has developed still allows us to grant them, no one is willing to make the effort, and the result is a feeling of unease that has led certain individuals to question the very use of these words, which are nonetheless perfectly French.

It is not possible to undertake a study of the words "culture" and "civilization" in a few paragraphs. It is scarcely even possible to summarize the stages through which these words have gone in the history of language and ideas, and the relations they entertain with comparable foreign expressions. "*Civilisation*" is a recent term in the French language. According to a remarkable study by Lucien Febvre that appeared in the publications of the Centre de Synthèse, it only occurs in print in 1766, and its invention can probably be attributed to

Baron d'Holbach.[3] At more or less the same date, the word *Kultur* appeared in the German language, and the English word "civilization" is found in 1772 in a text attributed to Dr. Johnson. This simultaneous act of creation, in which it is very difficult to know what role was played by borrowing, raises problems that cannot be dealt with in a few words. The most obvious one concerns the late date at which a word we can now no longer do without first appeared. Since the reality of civilization was just as undisputed and just as clearly experienced two centuries ago as it is today, why is the term so modern if the idea is so old?

A crude response to this question would propose two reasons. The first is that the old language had at its disposal at least three terms, and their use covered every eventuality. For example, the word "civility" was used to refer to an honest and gentle way of being and talking with others. "Politeness" was used to signify a developed culture offering the possibility of an affectionate and humane concern for others. Finally, the term "police" or "policed" signified, according to Furetière in 1690, "the order that must be observed for the sustaining and maintaining of States, the opposite of barbarity." These words, particularly the third of them, were used unproblematically for a long time, until the day when they no longer seemed to correspond to the precise meaning they had only ever expressed somewhat uneasily, and that was being imposed more and more clearly by the movement of ideas. There is no need to insist on the fact that "civilization" appears at the moment when the effort of the Encyclopedists is coming to fruition. The term is essentially a creation of Enlightenment philosophy. After some hesitations, it acquires the ideal meaning that belief in indefinite progress allows it to receive. At the end of the eighteenth century, civilization thus refers to the general universal model toward which all societies at the time appear to be tending. It is the mirror of the boundless perfection that a fanaticism of hope offers all mankind, with a naive and in some ways rather barbaric faith.

For almost fifty years this philosophy would appear to have barred writers from using the word "civilization" other than in the singular. You said "civilization"; "civilizations" was not recognized. It took the arrival of an author who has already been cited, Ballanche, for the word that had hitherto been destined to represent a single, ideal reality to acquire a plural form. "Slavery," writes Ballanche in *The Old Man and the Young Man*, "no longer exists save in the debris of ancient civilizations."[4] The change that this new usage entails is immediately apparent. The notion of civilization acquires a historical or ethnographical meaning. It is no longer a matter of evoking a human ideal, each society is acknowledged to have a certain number of specific defining features—material existence, social organization, intellectual life—and these characteristics are facts that no longer attract a value judgment. Civilization thus depends on history; it is on the verge of disappearing into different civilizations, being merely the life and death of all the truths that characterize the various human groups.

Meanwhile, what has become of the word *Kultur*? According to Tonnelat, the word is a direct version of the French word *culture*, which was used from the seventeenth century in an abstract sense, and from the beginning of the eighteenth *signified* the training of the mind. In Germany, Adelung's dictionary of 1774 records three meanings: the modern liberation of the mind (which is the meaning it retains in the expression *Kulturkampf*), a certain distinction and refinement of manner, and finally a social condition characterized by material well-being and political order. These ideas will soon receive from the Sturm und Drang writers an enrichment that will provide a starting point for the elaboration by philosophers of new intellectual processes. In the same way as Herder and Kant, Schiller will seek to define the various stages of *Kultur*, from the simple domestication of animals and the cultivation of the land to the establishment of forms of good government. Wilhelm von Humboldt distinguishes among the terms *Zivilisation*, *Kultur*, and *Bildung* (training or education), and this distinction expresses for the first time a conflict of meaning out of which two conceptions of the world will emerge. "Civilization" is that which, in the material domain and in the development of customs, tends to provide men with a gentler and more humane condition. "Culture" indicates that men, rising above utilitarian social considerations, have turned to the disinterested study of science and the arts. As for *Bildung*, it indicates a true state of intellectual and moral accomplishment.

The sudden change of sense that the word civilization has undergone by this stage is clearly visible. According to Humboldt's analysis, civilization has a sort of mechanical quality about it. It requires of the individual no conscious effort or any effort of will. It is enough to be born at a given moment of evolution to be able to enjoy its advantages. It is given; it is not acquired. *Kultur*, on the contrary, is *transbiologisch*. It presupposes a personal struggle against nature. It is the act of awareness through which each individual, in contact with the habits of the community, seeks to fulfill himself by acquiring the disciplines that will allow him to dominate the world. Finally, *Bildung* is associated with a number of particularly gifted individuals and reflects their vocation as leaders. The latter meaning contains the seeds of the thinking of the German Romantics, that of Fichte in particular. Fichte it is who develops the notion of a typical culture that, backed by the power of the state and that of religion, must serve as a model for other national cultures. In other words, just as certain individuals have a mission that derives from the perfection of their development, so certain nations have a supreme duty to represent to others the ideal that is referred to by the term *Humanität*. For Fichte, it is Germany who must provide the intellectual leadership and the political leadership of Europe.

However hasty and superficial they are, these remarks do bring out the general direction in which the words have evolved. The meaning of the French term *civilisation* and that of the German term *Kultur* gradually undergo a restriction of their field as history provides a better definition of the

domains to which they apply. Having signified a universal
ideal, *civilisation* ends up referring, in the hands of sociolo-
gists, to the material and moral modes of action of any human
community. *Kultur*, as Tonnelat quite rightly notes, loses all
general significance and comes to represent the intellectual
achievements not of humanity as a whole, but of a specific
state whose exclusive property they remain. This specific point
is significant, and it has much more far-reaching consequences
for the German term than for the French one. It may even be
observed that the word "civilization" has retained an exemplary significance, specific to it and present at its origin, and
this makes it a quite different term from the word *Kultur*. In
the vocabulary of French, the word *civilisation* is always to be
found alongside *civilisations*, and if it no longer expresses an
ideal of progress guaranteed to humanity simply by virtue of
its development, it continues to refer to a point of perfection,
a favorable moment in time when, thanks to a heritage of
magnificent traditions and the creative effort of certain individuals, a store of supremely balanced moral and intellectual
riches is entrusted to politically prosperous societies.

Through its nuances and its character, in which refinement,
taste, and subtle instinct play an important part, the word
civilisation is deeply imbued with the habits of the French
mind. It is in that sense that Nietzsche's celebrated remark to
Strindberg in a letter of 1888 should be understood: "There is
no other civilization save that of France. This is incontrovertible. It stands to reason, she is of necessity the only true one."
The word *culture*, on the other hand, because of the attraction
exerted by the comparable German word, sometimes seems
rather less at home in our language, as if it reflected a foreign
notion rather than a set of forms acceptable to our tradition.
That is no doubt a vague and superficial impression. "Culture" belongs intimately to our language, and in its various
meanings it expresses those values that are most familiar to
our minds. In general, culture is the set of means that are
required to prepare men to understand civilization and reap

all of its benefits. Culture is only meaningful in relation to civilization. It marks the point where an individual makes contact with the heritage that is his and appropriates it for himself. Goethe, who steered clear of any Romantic form of expression, saw in culture a link between nature and art. In a rather different spirit, it can be said that culture is the means whereby man gains access actively and consciously to civilization. This is a glorious pathway on which man learns to master the treasures he received naturally as his birthright. But it is also fraught with danger, since in the course of this personal journey, led astray by the abuses of science and other intellectual disciplines, he runs the risk of losing the world he had first discovered.

—July 31, 1941

In Praise of Rhetoric

The lawyer Maurice Garçon has just written a book about eloquence and the law in which, adding to its other merits, he takes advantage of the opportunity to forget that he is an orator.[1] The style he uses, the form of thinking he employs, and the aversion he displays for arguments that are too simple, make his book a work that is free of any trace of eloquence, and one that is written entirely by a writer. This is a delightful quality. It is tempting to think that the author of such a book needed to be the most brilliant of lawyers in order to write it; but it is even more gratifying to realize that in writing it, he forgot what he was. There is nothing more dismal than an orator whose only medium for thinking about himself is the oratorical style.

This book is more of a treatise than an essay. It has none of the severity of a technical work, but it does have its rigor, its thoughtful precision, and its abstract dignity. It is a book without anecdotes, in which one or two portraits in the style of La Bruyère provide examples rather than a diversion. Maurice Garçon looks in turn at the training of a lawyer, the lessons provided him by the classics, the procedures he employs and every form of language, from preamble to peroration, leaving out none of resources that the true orator can find in study and reflection. The rules he sets out are very general, but they express precise principles and a powerful intellectual method: that provided by the possession of an entirely classical culture.

Maurice Garçon observes very pertinently that in an age when speech has acquired such importance, nothing is done to teach the art of oratory. Whether it be it the judge who is called on to pass sentence or the lawyer called on to plead a case, none of those whose profession requires them to give oral expression to their thoughts receives any instruction in how to speak. In schools, no attention is paid to developed argument, even in the written form. In law school, no heed is paid to rhetoric and its rules. In the law courts, the way trainee lawyers are taught to plead [*dans les conférences du stage*] is a sham exercise overseen by no competent person, which provides the novice with a feeling of self-assurance rather than a desire to know the rules. Basically, there is no such thing as an impartial mentor. The lawyer receives no assistance from his peers.[2] All that the press ever shows him is indifference, smug goodwill, or disdainful criticism. Common sense has to make up for all that is missing.

One of the most interesting things about Maurice Garçon's book is that in it, he makes no secret of his attachment to the study of rhetoric, and to a knowledge of the ancient rhetoricians and the orators of antiquity. He speaks of the works of Quintilian and Cicero as one who owes them more than just principles, and he has written pages on the art of Gorgias that are perfectly evenhanded. It is a fact that ancient rhetoric transformed effects and processes that seemed to have taken shape haphazardly deep in the soul into a studied method and a conscious system. It would accept nothing that was not calculated. It believed that the orator must at no time break free of the rules governing every action that influences the public, and that instinct can never adequately replace the patient study of these ballistics. This is a perennial truth. We have nothing to fear from excessive thought. If voice is the basis and condition of a literature of eloquence, if what an audience will accept and require defines the structure and the length of a work, these forms are all the more closely dependent on a well-prepared plan, an awareness of the rules, and the organization of a style. In so far as improvisation plays a part in any given art, that improvisation must be concerted, what is impromptu must be organized, and the artist must keep chance in check using a system of disciplines of a higher order.

Maurice Garçon's book contains some gloomy reflections on the fate of the orator, who instantly perishes each time he encounters silence. But there is no cause for an author to be gloomy when the art of oratory has provided him with both ephemeral success and an enduring work. For even those who dislike eloquence will take pleasure in reading this book, which takes it as its subject while containing almost none of it.

—August 1, 1941

A View of Descartes

Paul Valéry was destined to write a book on Descartes. It has always been clear that it is precisely because he hates philosophy that he is drawn to the supreme philosopher. He has published a declaration of disdain for all forms of metaphysics, and a series of admiring statements about the father of modern metaphysics. The latter was merely a fragment consisting of one or two pages. The study he has just written provides the introduction to a set of extracts from Descartes's work published in Corrêa's "Immortal Pages" collection, and it is much more substantial.[1] It provides a set of profound ideas, if not about Descartes himself, then about the relations between Paul Valéry and Descartes.

As one might imagine, this study by Paul Valéry is not a philosophical interpretation but an enquiry into a particular structure of the mind. This as we know is one of his major preoccupations, one that drove him to write not only his celebrated meditation on the method of Leonardo da Vinci, as well as *Monsieur Teste*, but also numerous thoughts with which he remains unwaveringly obsessed. Such single-mindedness could not fail to lead him to Descartes's door. Necessarily written into his reveries there was a repeated return to this thinker, the form of whose thinking, independent of its content, presupposes an extraordinary enigma that appears to belong not to one man, but to the mind itself. He would seem to have gone in search of himself in the mystery of a perfectly self-controlled, precise, and yet confused intelligence, going out to meet the obscure consciousness at the heart of any true work of the intellect, enquiring into his own thought in the process of enquiring into this superior individual, and in the end discovering himself proudly and humbly in the guise of a great philosopher.

An appropriation of this kind, which seemed to confirm that Descartes had always been held in reserve for him, explains how eagerly awaited these pages were which he was destined to write. So great was this expectation that it undoubtedly explains why it continues unabated once these pages have been read. The thought comes to mind that Paul Valéry's Descartes has still to be written, that if it ever were written then there could be nothing more important or more original, but that this will probably never happen, since the secret of each of these minds is only destined to reveal itself to the other in a mirage in which both of them cease to be visible.

What Paul Valéry has brought to light with the power and brilliance that are naturally his, is a rather visible version of Descartes, showing his proud superiority and the force of character that made him ground all certainty in a certainty about himself. What enchants us about him, says Valéry, and brings him alive for us, however outmoded his work may be, is his consciousness of self, a consciousness of his resources, a consciousness of an attention in which is concentrated everything that he is, a consciousness that is so complete and so supreme that it makes his Self an instrument whose infallibility is on a par with the consciousness he has of that self. The *cogito ergo sum* is only meaningful in relation to this "I" that he invokes and puts to work. The interest we may continue to take in this "I" has nothing to do with some philosophical significance or other (Paul Valéry denies all such significance rather brazenly), but with its role as an interpellator and a stimulant for the mind of Descartes himself. It represents, supremely forcefully, an appeal the power of pride. It calls on all the resources of his being to awaken. It indicates that the "I," because it is Descartes's "I," is the only mode of access to ways of thinking that are absolutely general and rigorously pure. The *cogito* is the most audacious dramatic coup through which a philosopher has ever deliberately and openly established his Self as a system of reference for the world and a fount of creative reform.

As methods, both systematic doubt and the tabula rasa can be interpreted perfectly from that point of view. It is reasonable for this Self that is so conscious of its demands and of the rule it discovers within itself to want to rid itself of all the difficulties or parasitical notions that have obscured it historically; it is necessary for it to become blind, deaf and insensitive to anything that risks contradicting its own order; it must necessarily deny the obsessions, the illusory entities, and the obstacles that weigh it down, dim its natural light, and prevent it from reaching the pinnacle of its intellectual vigor. Descartes's will drives him to reject fundamentally everything that would prevent him from making best use of his intelligence, and on the contrary to develop everything that accords with the fertility of his mind and allows him to make the most magnificent use of it. Descartes's Self is a geometer. Consequently, each time he can respond to the problems he encounters through the exercise of this tried and tested self, he triumphs, and in order to increase his dominion over phenomena, he constantly seeks to apply the organized consciousness he calls his method, and that ultimately conquers for him a limitless domain. His self commands him to do everything or to redo everything. His inventiveness competes with what is most singular and diverse in life. He advances by creating himself and creating everything from himself. He is victorious

wherever he struggles with nature. He succumbs only when
he tackles the false problems of tradition.

Such a view of Descartes is undeniably very plausible, and
it is much more directly related to traditional Cartesian analysis than Paul Valéry seems to realize. Philosophers and histori-
ans have long since included Descartes's own procedures in
their interpretations of Cartesianism as a real element, and not
just an explicatory factor. They too have admired this superior
consciousness, this extraordinary will to power that expressed
itself through neither passion nor anguish but through
supreme serenity of vision, implacable self-assurance, and
unfailingly reflective and methodical progression. They have
laid stress on the intervention of this "I," which, with inimitable serenity, imposes its presence for the first time on the theater of the mind, delivering the most personal of monologues
and through that monologue, obliging us to be ourselves, to
rediscover each detail of our discussions and doubts, and giving us access to the universal in the pure intimacy of its speech.
There is thus nothing that is not legitimate about Paul Valéry's
examination, or about his wish to reach the mind of Descartes
through Cartesian philosophy. It is not so much his examination or its conclusions that perhaps surprise us as the limits
within which his conclusions confine a system of thought that
is so enigmatic that it remains so even in what is supremely
clear about it.

The intimate structure of Descartes's mind is almost impossible to approach. Karl Jaspers, who devoted a ferociously critical book to it a few years ago, remarked that the strangest of
contrasts made it inaccessible.[2] At first, Descartes's work
appears totally clear and open, but this openness is allied with
a power of fascination and seduction that we unwarily and
indiscriminately obey. It appears designed to be accessible to
everyone thanks to a language that is admirably simple and
free, and at the same time it betrays a highly aristocratic
reserve on its author's part, and is in fact addressed to a mere
handful of reasonable individuals, setting an example that others are not invited to follow. It has always been understood

that in Descartes there lay concealed a mystery, but the mask behind which he advances is undoubtedly something quite different from the expression of piety and faith that a rationalist philosopher would have adopted in order to defy the fanaticism of his times. Descartes is not just impenetrable because of his prudence, but for reasons that have to do with the nature of his mind, and result from a fascinating ambiguity peculiar to him.

As many commentators have remarked, this spirit, whose general air seems to be one of serenity, evenness of pace, and careful, confident deliberation, in fact has a liking for surprises, and is undaunted by unforeseen consequences. His singular, brutal, and violent character transforms his thinking, even though it has been completely purified, into a series of shows of force that never flinch at the absurd. His serenity is the symbol of a passion that outdoes the most extraordinary flights of the soul in its desire for supremacy and its will to power. The purely rational claims he makes on knowledge ground his philosophy not only in an intellectual dimension, but also in a mystical purpose that is vouched for in his biography. Descartes is a man who, at the very moment of discovering the principles of universal knowledge, was having dreams that he attributed to an evil genius, and who called on God, the Virgin Mary, and his faith to endorse a discovery that stemmed from his faith in himself.

Drawn to the disquieting nature of these enigmas, Karl Jaspers tried to give a symbolic representation of them. He wondered whether the clarity of Cartesian reason was not overshadowed by the form of a dark genius. For what is Descartes's mind if not thought itself which, through its very purity, its universalizing ambition and its detachment from history, has become a sort of elemental force, akin to the blind vitality of nature, a vitality that appears to the observer as either bungling and devoid of sense, or filled with sense and replete with possibilities? It consists, Jaspers goes on, of a subterranean force that has managed to become identical with empty reason but has not attained any human dignity and is passionately in search of it, veering from true because of its exactness, and either falling short of humanity or overshooting it through too complete an identification with mankind's essential power. Descartes could in that case be described as a human being who, without noticing it, has never quite managed to catch up with himself.

It goes without saying that the only value of such an interpretation is that it brings out the insuperable nature of the enigma rather than providing an explanation for it. For if Descartes's mind can offer an insight into a sort of "prehuman" life of man, as Jaspers claims, it gives the even greater impression of a total human being, an accomplished aristocrat whose authority comes just as much from disdain as it does from power, and who obliges the history he has rejected to follow in his steps. The enigma of Descartes is probably visible in the portraits of him. People have described the diffident grandeur of that figure, the haughty power of his attention. The absence of all reverie is itself far less a sign of indifference toward the world of dream than the sign of a sleeper who, through an admirable effort, has succeeded in transcending his dream and transforming it into a brilliant, self-conscious fancy.

—August 11–12, 1941

A Novel by Mauriac

The latest novel by François Mauriac, *A Woman of the Phari-sees*, is quite remarkable.[1] It contains all the refinements of a patiently honed technique. It reveals the efforts of the novelist to conceal the difficulties that beset him. He gives the impression of being someone perfectly aware of his weaknesses, and intent on responding to them with increasingly well-adapted and ever more ambiguous stratagems. Reading the book is like reading it backward. Not with the feeling that it is coming together, but with the impression that is coming apart beneath the gaze that seeks to penetrate it too inquisitively. This is quite an exciting spectacle. It provides pleasures that make up for those we generally ask of books, and which they rarely provide.

A Woman of the Pharisees is a story told by a man who witnessed the events it contains when he was thirteen, and who says "I." It is thus not a tale in which the writer can intervene directly. It is a true story whose truth is that of a storyteller who is himself a character in a novel. What does a novelist achieve by making use of a procedure that excludes

him in certain respects from his work and lets him keep control of it only through an intermediary? He is obliged to
refrain from substituting his own vision for that of the storyteller he has chosen to take his place, and who necessarily has
only a limited and subjective knowledge of events. Whereas
the novelist, according to a highly ambiguous convention, lays
claim to limitless powers of indiscretion over the characters
and the story itself, the character who says "I" is restored to
the usual conditions that apply in life. Not only does he inter-
pret facts with the judgment with which he is provided, he
can also inevitably know only part of them. He remains outside them, and what he perceives of them is an expression of
himself much more than a precise revelation of things themselves. Last, he is not in a position to have seen everything,
heard everything, and understood everything. The self-
indulgence of the devil upon two sticks who lifts the roofs of
houses is strictly denied him.[2]

These remarks obviously apply to the traditional form of
the novel. There is no question of any other form with Mauriac, who has sometimes struggled dangerously with himself in
order to remain faithful to it but has never resigned himself to
breaking free of it. This type of novel, as is well known, is
governed by verisimilitude, the imitation of reality, and the
faithful reflection of character types that can be encountered
in real life. From time to time, Mauriac seems more concerned
to create a world rather than mimic the appearance of the one
to which an entirely external psychology consigns us. But he
is swiftly brought back to the usual conventions. He submits
to them without respecting them. He seeks them out and flees
them at the same time. Finally, he retains merely the most
superficial element to be found in them, the one that restricts
him most and is least able to delude us. There is no doubt
that it is to this obscure struggle between an instinctively subjective form of creation and a concern for psychological realism that Mauriac owes the strangely arbitrary appearance of
some of his characters and some of his books. His wish is to

include in his work only totally objective dramas, and beings capable of wandering back and forth unchanged between his books and real life. But his pleasure lies in devouring his creatures and reducing them to himself. He behaves toward them like a God who interferes constantly in their nature, making them act in accordance with his ways rather than with their own reality and leading them toward their fates with an astonishing lack of restraint. He creates them, then he strikes them down with his decisions. By the way he behaves toward his characters, he seems to be trying constantly to give mankind an example of the behavior that, according to him, is that of God himself, whose grace is all-powerful.

In a book like *A Woman of the Pharisees*, where the novelist is supposed not to intervene, what will Mauriac do? One gains the impression that, aware of the dangerous temptation that can lead him to act too complacently in his characters' stead, he has tried to take away all of his power by delegating it to the storyteller who represents him. His novel is more or less a closed book for him. He is of necessity absent from it. He willingly condemns himself to impotence. He plays a trick on himself by depriving himself of himself. Henceforth, how will he exercise that jurisdiction over his story and his characters which seems essential to his authoritarian pride as a writer? Unfortunately, the situation is an awkward one, difficulties abound and with each new episode the pitfalls become more serious. And in order to maintain contact with the world he wishes to reveal, Mauriac resorts to a strategy of verisimilitude that is remarkable in every respect.

As its title suggests, *A Woman of the Pharisees* is the story of a woman of means who is not only more aware of other people's faults than she is of her own, but has a domineering urge to provide spiritual guidance, and who is transformed through the rigor she displays into an intense power of judgment and condemnation in relation to others. Ruin and misery pile up all around her. She sees evil where it is present, attracts it where it is not, and boasts of disasters she has foreseen even

when by foreseeing them she has partly been their cause. She
is thus the triumphant witness of her own indignation. She
drives her husband to despair by convincing him that his first
wife is worthless. She perturbs the lives of two children by
accusing them of impure acts of which they are completely
unaware. She makes the lives of a couple a misery because she
is appalled at their spiritual decadence, even though only she
can see it. And finally she denounces a noble and worthy priest
to his superiors, as a condemnation for acting according to a
deeper purpose, whereas she herself is woefully in thrall to the
world. All of these tragedies, with their complex intellectual
structure, revolve around a thirteen-year-old witness whose
task is to ensure that we are fully informed about them, and
who does indeed carry out his task with formidable diligence.
Not only is he to be found wherever the drama surfaces, not
only has he retained every detail of the facts and every word
of the conversations in his monstrously infallible memory, but
he also succeeds in reporting events he can never have known,
and revealing their dramatic development as if he had been in
control of them as well as being their witness. What a strange
and fabulous privilege! The character who says "I" is a demi-
urge who thinks he is a powerful writer of novels.

Unsurprisingly, given his concern for verisimilitude and for
the structure of his narratives, Mauriac offers various reasons
to justify such a privilege and explain this unbelievable gift for
being well informed. There is nothing more fascinating than
to watch him struggle to preserve a degree of authenticity for
his methods. He displays extraordinary skill and relentless
ingenuity. Never have the characters in a novel had such a
predilection for notes, confidential messages, and notebooks,
which fate eventually hands over obligingly to the storyteller.
Never have heroes listened so much at doors, even when this
habit is consistent neither with their character not the requirements of their role. Remarks such as this one regularly occur:
"Without Michèle I would perhaps never have known about
the early flare-up of the drama. . . . Even though she was the

most candid of children . . . she would continuously observe Brigitte Plan." Or else there are remarks that explain the urge that the actors of the drama feel to tell all in the presence of an innocent child: "I do not believe," says the witness, "that many children can have been chosen by grown-ups to be their adjudicator as often as I was." Or else this sentence, which is a real gem: "It may perhaps be thought that in opening his heart in this way to a boy who was not quite seventeen, Father Calou proved that he had not made much progress so far in matters of sound judgment." Occasionally finding himself short of tricks, the novelist himself preempts the objections that the reader may be tempted to raise, and presents him with some curious challenges. "Someone asks me," he writes, "how do you know about all these events when you weren't present when they happened? By what right do you repeat conversations you haven't heard?" And the storyteller, admitting defeat, gives this proud reply in which all concern for objectivity has finally vanished: "I have no doubt exercised my right to organize this material and orchestrate this reality, this enduring life that will only die when I do."

A novelist can do whatever he wants; he is the master of his conventions, his extravagances and his laws, but on one condition: he must in every case submit to a genuine necessity that he consolidates in the course of obeying it. Mauriac too does what he wants, but he piles on the excuses so as to convince people that he is not doing what he wants, that he is a slave to reality, that he is dependent on his characters, that he is the prisoner of his narrative. To a casual observer he gives the impression of being faithful to the obscure nature of the beings he has created. But a more careful examination reveals him to be the most indiscreet of novelists, the least inhibited by the limits of his characters, and the most capable, at any moment, of lending them his gaze, his voice or his total knowledge of the book of which they are merely a part. What happens to the *Woman of the Pharisees* in this book devoted to her? One day, this proud woman, who makes demands only on others and is content for her part to adapt her behavior in a purely external way to the rule she has chosen, finally has doubts about her own virtue. Having spent her life seeing only the edifying side of her actions, she gradually begins to see their imperfect, even horrifying nature. She is overtaken by scruples. These Furies of the Christian world deliver her up to a judgment of extreme rigor. She undergoes various ordeals. She discovers the world and likes it. She becomes perfect the more she leaves behind the appearance of perfection. The final paragraph of the novel begins with this sentence: "I realized that she had become detached even from her sins, and that she was leaving everything up to Mercy."

There is no need to dwell on the arbitrary nature of this outcome. It is a tradition with Mauriac. What is more remarkable is the extreme care with which the author prepares and defends his conclusion. In lengthy analyses, he attempts to justify these unforeseeable transformations and make them natural and satisfying for the mind. All is explained, all is clear. Everything happens in a reasonable order. Not a single doubt can be raised that the author has not foreseen and allayed. As a result, the verisimilitude of the character remains intact, but it is also without importance. It has all the interest of a coherent theory. It reveals the consciousness of the writer, his interest in psychological development, his urge to be a director of souls that makes him guide these wretched creatures toward redemption. But this verisimilitude gives no authenticity to the world whose fundamental characteristic it appears to be. It makes us neither curious to believe nor blind to what is unbelievable. It leaves us as dissatisfied with the inner development of the character as we are satisfied with the author who has explained it to us.

By the end of *A Woman of the Pharisees*, it is clear that Mauriac has destroyed verisimilitude by the excessive and detailed nature of his explanations and rescued it with a few details that can be explained by his own nature. There is a character in the novel whose mysterious quality is occasionally quite fascinating. It is the storyteller himself, this child about whom we know little, who seems racked by obscure passions, who hovers around the drama of the other characters with a peculiar relish and over whom the shadow of a cruel and thwarted fate constantly hangs. What will he become? What enigmas lie in wait for him? We are all the more interested in his story for being indifferent to the one he tells, and we create him out of all of the attention we refuse to give to the over-drawn characters who make up the novel.

—August 18–19, 1941

Young Novelists

Several novels by young novelists are currently available. These works, which have just appeared, and which reflect an art that is still in its infancy, offer few insights into the future of the novel itself. Rather, they are proof that novelists of talent who are capable of achieving a certain level of self-expression, seem naturally to accept the habits and conventions of a genre that seeks in vain, from those who approach it, some modicum of pride, some capacity for technical innovation, even some sense of adventure and experiment. How do they go about their work? They are given a number of set rules that they do not question, and they stick to them solely because it is customary to do so. And if they deviate from them it is even worse, for this break with convention appears to come not from some deeper imperative but from an ignorant rejection of the usual practices, without any understanding of why they deserved to be rejected. That the novel is an extremely difficult art form, in which, before inventing anything else, the novelist must first invent strict rules, and in which he is tyrannically dependent upon a form that he has provided for himself, is something that no author appears to be aware of, attracted as each one is by the freedom he enjoys and the interest of the subject he is developing.

These remarks would seem particularly apt in the case of Raymond Guérin's book *When the End Comes*.[1] It has great qualities, substantial ambition, and a reasonably strong sense of the requirements of its subject, and yet it swings perilously between opposing versions of itself that do not cohere. The novel tells the story of a man who is obsessed by a desire to know what sort of person his father was. He gathers evidence, episodes, and details. He desperately seeks out everything there is to know about him, and he speaks of him with extraordinarily violent realism, as if the crudest of details have become sacred for him through the light that they shed on the mystery that must be probed. What is there to know about this unfathomable individual who seems to withhold himself through his very banality? How can he be reached, how can it be sure that he really was the man he appears to be? What is there to remember about his life? All is obscurity and dark secret.

Raymond Guérin appears to have had the idea of expressing this impression through a twofold contrast. First, he implies that the son, consumed by a desire to know his progenitor, is guided in this project by a vague hatred, an unutterable contempt that is vainly in search of a justification. It is tempting to imagine that beneath this passion for knowledge, this yearning for candor that gives rise to a realism of considerable cruelty, there lies a harrowingly severe and vengeful sentiment. Nothing could be farther from the truth. It gradually becomes clear that in describing a coarse and vulgar man, incapable of nobility and driven by a brutish appetite for work and money, this implacable son is describing the man he loves most, and both respects and admires. His determination to say everything is merely a determination to say also what he loves. The analysis he brings to bear on his father, the grotesque descriptions of him that he provides, the stories in which he shows him having to cope with the most humiliating of illnesses, are all the inventions of an affection that is endlessly caught up in a debate with itself. Everything is grist for its mill, and everything poses a threat to it. It thrives on what consumes it and reduces it to naught.

The other contrast, which Raymond Guérin has set up even more consciously, comes from the mystery he discovers in a man whom he describes as rather lacking in mystery. Who is this character we come up against as if he were enigma itself? He is a man who has been a wigmaker, a soldier, and a head-waiter, who has worked tirelessly throughout his life, who seems never to have had a dream, who has never asked himself any questions, who was unaware of the life he lived and indifferent to it, and who dies having obtained nothing save his own annihilation, in a degrading agony that he endures while deriving nothing from it. Was that what he was? Was he not something else? Have appearances not betrayed him? Is a more profound interpretation not possible? What is there to say? Is he not being credited with too many thoughts? In his search for the truth about his father, the son performs a sort of tireless dance around this shadow, which he pursues in vain. Deep down, man is impenetrable; beings live only through the portraits that other men provide of them, and those portraits are imaginary.

A few years ago, Raymond Guérin, whose second book this is, wrote the sad tale of a couple as seen from the perspective of one of the spouses. This careful, precise story, entitled *Zobain*, had all the appearance of accuracy, but was destined eventually to appear to us as false.[2] In all its completeness and truthfulness, the analysis was merely a distorting mirror in which anyone it reflected appeared not as he was, but as the version of himself that he concealed. Clearly, he has taken as his subject the same myth of existence this time, though in another form. And he pursues it with the same severity, the same dramatic hesitation between hatred and friendship and the same wish to deceive himself with the breadth of his knowledge and the power of his insight. Unfortunately, these qualities disappear in a book where in the end, what predominates is a realist narrative, overburdened with descriptions whose only justification is themselves, and driven by a desire to provide a true-to-life picture of insignificant events. We cannot know whether Guérin has stuck closely to a model drawn from life, but he constantly gives the impression that the portrait he must provide is deflecting him entirely away from the intentions that this portrait should reveal. Gone is any sense of the drama of a project that can only be spoiled by its fulfillment, that desperate pursuit of an elusive truth, that effort to capture the only images of a man one has loved that could save him from oblivion, even if those images are ugly and vulgar. All that we can see are the twists and turns of a narrative that seems drawn from the most familiar reality, and whose origins give it a remarkable veneer of truth and a real absence of purpose.

Guérin's talents truly deserve our attention. They must even be quite considerable, since they have allowed him to write a work that is coherent and complete, even if it has little in common with the work he proposed to write, and whose phantom is visible from time to time. Something rather different can be said about Paul Gadenne's novel *Siloé*, a large book of four hundred pages that is so likeable that it would be good to be able to say only positive things about it.[3] But the fact remains that this considerable effort, which is the fruit of patient energy, extreme spiritual ambition, and all the striving of a soul in search of itself, is almost nullified by the inconsistent use it makes of the novel form, and the weaknesses of its method. Whereas *When the End Comes* offers an example of a book that is transformed by its use of a form to which it does not itself correspond, and is thus effectively betrayed by its very qualities, *Siloé* is an example of a work in which ambitious designs, stubborn effort, and the strivings of sensibility fail to impress, for want of any strictly literary purpose and any genuine intellectual vigilance. It would appear that for Gadenne, as indeed for numerous others, a novel is not a problem, and that it therefore exists from the moment every-thing that can be written and imagined about a great subject has been assembled. Narrative sweep and ample food for thought—ultimately there would appear to be no need for anything else.

The error of this writer is all the more glaring in that he has chosen as his subject one that calls for the greatest possible literary attention. *Siloé* is the same story with which Thomas Mann composed *The Magic Mountain*. It is a tale of transfor-mation. A young student who has hitherto known only the frantic life of competitive examinations falls ill, and in the mountain sanatorium where he goes for treatment he dis-covers a new life whose meaning he gradually becomes aware of. Initially, he turns in on himself. During a solitary period of lengthy repose, he learns the importance of a form of time of which he was unaware. By contemplating nature and find-ing that it is both totally alien to him and intimately close, he uncovers the existence of a world that no description can exhaust, and of which only the signs are visible. A semimythi-cal liaison with a girl helps him understand how mysterious and profound the destiny is of a man who becomes aware of the double and triple universe in which his life is traced out, and who, like someone born blind who miraculously regains his sight, goes back to where he came from and finally sees things as they are.

It is clear that Gadenne's book is the story of a nascent spiritual vocation. It is the adventure of a mind. There are few external events. The occasional characters whom we meet and who are not without interest are not destined to breathe life into the world they inhabit, but rather serve to enlighten the hero about himself. Everything takes place through internal descriptions, psychological to-and-fro, recurrent thoughts and attempts at reflection. The book is a series of cordial encoun-ters with objects and people who reveal themselves only gradu-ally. The mountain, the torrent, a tree, winter and spring are lures for an absolute that remains always invisible. Love leads the individual toward contact with living shadows where he becomes one with the true rhythm of nature. Page after page, with the most creditable lack of any urge to please, with powerful gravity and eloquence, the author seeks to take us to those regions in which his emotion began. He tries to rediscover the paths that led him to a horizon filled with wonders. He is put off neither by the difficulty of his task nor by the inadequacies of art. He struggles and he triumphs, at least on his own count.

What is missing from such a work? Whatever is missing when a work exists only as an intention. One or two pages are quite moving, and the book as a whole creates an impression of substance thanks to the scope it requires. But where is the book itself? Where is the form, the structure that would allow it to represent the mysterious world into which it seeks to lure us? There is no trace of the intellectual effort that in advance, as its reflections progressed, would have eliminated naivety of thinking and innocent reverie. And we are carried along by an eloquent confusion that constantly loses sight of its object, or else only catches up with it by resorting to trivial images contained within a banality of expression that proves a sad betrayal of an author who is otherwise extremely demanding.

—September 18, 1941

Theater and the Public

Jacques Copeau has just brought out an important essay on popular theater in the People's Library collection.[1] Part of his study concerns theater in general. Another is particularly concerned with a type of theater that has been given various names, and that has recently been called theater for the masses. Serious attention must be given to what a mind like Jacques Copeau's may think about the confused state of current drama, and the illusory hopes designed to restore it to a life it no longer has. The same thoughts can be applied to any art. The dangers arising from current circumstances are negligible, provided they find no succor in the usual prejudices of intelligence and sentiment.

Jacques Copeau's study is not systematic. It is made up of a series of reflections, some concerning the past and some the present. What was theater like in earlier times? There was an age when the people came together as a group, in theatrical celebrations that organized legend and history and were a manifestation of the higher world of the gods. There was another age when unnumbered crowds, inspired by great faith, came from far and wide to attend performances lasting hours and sometimes days, put on by an entire city and concerned with the essence of their spiritual lives. Closer to us, another type of theater based on a solid notion of man succeeded in maintaining the necessary relations with the moral life of a people, appealing to natural man and his passions, religious man and his obligations, and social man and his conventions. Classical theater, like Greek or medieval theater, was possible only because there existed a public whose boundaries had not been destroyed by a negative philosophy, and whose inclinations encountered in irrefutable laws that resistance without which passions lose all dramatic dignity.

Copeau has no difficulty in extracting from a few observations about contemporary society some remarks that allow him to explain the shortcomings of current theater. "The nature of the public, its scale and its outlook—that," he writes, "is essentially the main issue when we consider the problem of theater." And he adds that if we are to restore a human art of drama that will set out the limits of man, the scope of his actions and the sense of his destiny, this will ultimately require a return to the deepest levels of ambition, truth and spiritual reflection. Nonetheless, setting aside these general conditions (about which moreover much would need to be said, and which lend themselves to very different interpretations), some form of renovation and some critical effort are not impossible. Jacques Copeau himself has constantly provided an example of personal effort met with unrivaled success, and though he has no illusions about the results he has achieved, he has singled out a number of ideas that indicate in what spirit future experiments should be carried out. The first reform he proposes is the creation of a center for theater culture. "Experience allows me to claim," he says, "that what French actors lack most of all today is a theater culture. Its influence can be felt neither at the Conservatoire nor in State Theaters as far as I can see. Yet that culture is what provides a guarantee against bad acting, and instills respect for the craft of theater, for the great masters and the great works." He is keen to emphasize that art and craft are not separate things. Great vocations cannot do without training. This is only detrimental to them if the training is mediocrely provided, with the sole aim of producing artificial talents. Copeau dwells at length on the importance of these reforms. It is remarkable that circumstance should make such a paean to skill seem necessary, as if actors, imitating authors, seemed happier to pay vague lip service to artistic method rather than learn how to master it.

Another of Copeau's remarks is directed at writers. In 1910 some of them were already attempting to renew the theater. They wanted to provide it with a basis that was literary, ideological, human, and more real. But it did not occur to them that dramatic form itself might change. They inherited a set form, which they accepted unquestioningly from their predecessors, and tried naïvely to breathe into plays constructed according to nineteenth-century bourgeois norms the new life offered by more authentic subjects, or subjects more likely to reach out to a wider public. Today what is clear is that the means of expression must perish along with the subjects they are attached to. The search for artistic means has become the great task of every creator. The invention of a form is the primary impulse behind his ambition. He knows intimately that he must only think of a work in terms of its means and on the basis of its means, and that on the contrary, to approach the creation of a work by way of a subject, or an effect imagined independently of its form, is to condemn yourself to aimless reverie.

What will be the form that will allow the theater to rediscover the object that eludes it, and to rise above the anomalies, curiosities, and peculiarities in which it now vainly goes in search of itself? Copeau displays extreme caution, of course, and rejects premature fiats as firmly as he does rigid ideologies and slavish imitations. His study of the various attempts at breathing life into the theater through the creation of a popular theater brings out the failures to which these experiments led. The theater of the French Revolution left not a single trace in any work, and eventually gave rise to vaudeville. The experiments that were carried out at the beginning of the century, prompted by Romain Rolland, did not attract a regular audience and gave satisfaction only to a few theorists whose minds were already made up. As for the efforts of the Popular Front, they were a pretext for futile commotion and left behind not the faintest glimmer of new hope. In the end, Jacques Copeau's preference seems to lie with a return to primitive conditions, a renewal of inner forces that will take place according to him on condition that a spirit of new birth and innocence can prevail. If popular theater, he writes, is called on to be born healthy and to live a pure life, it will need to go back, on its own terms, over the entire path and relive all the experience of the past. It will have to reinvent its form according to its needs and to the capacities of the public, and not laboriously apply readymade formulas to the construction of bogus ancient drama, fake classical tragedies, and false Shakespearian plays.

Jacques Copeau refers in this conclusion to popular theater, but his remarks clearly apply to theater in general, and would be meaningless if they only concerned the invention of one particular dramatic form, as defined by the quantity or the quality of the public. Indeed one of the implicit conclusions of his study is that there is no such thing as popular theater. The theater is linked in its goals and in its action to the existence of a public. The spectator is part of the play, not episodically or through a sort of necessary chance, as the reader is for the book that he picks up, but in an essential way, since the existence of the dramatic work depends on his presence and his participation. There is no need to dwell on these principles of the art of theater. Manifestly, the basic law of theater is that it should cause the spectator to identify and become one with someone on the stage; to become aware, through this identification, of life and death as realities held in common; finally, to feel indirectly that this common destiny joins him to all those around him, as they participate in the same anguish or the same joy. Such is the glory and the servitude of dramatic art. And it is what makes its situation a perilous one. The theater welcomes into both its intimacy and its structure an outsider who ends up playing a role in the creative act. This outsider, who is a spectator, must be as close as possible to man himself, without too much attention to issues of time, place, or class. If he belongs to too precise a social or political category, he obliges the author either to portray only a certain category of men or else, in what amounts to the death of art, to give his work an external goal, be it political, social, or religious. Theater necessarily presupposes the public in its entirety; in other words the greatest number possible; in other words and in short: man alone.

What could a popular theater possibly be? If the idea is to imagine an art form that would not appeal to a particular class, namely the poorest or least cultivated one, that would not even appeal to the crowd considered as a compromise between the elite and the mass, but would give itself the goal of reaching out to every man, every public, and involving them intimately in the revelation of a secret, which is the essence of art, there is nothing for it but to invent theater in all of its purity and authenticity. Either popular theater is merely a deviation, the enslavement of art to propaganda purposes, or else it is a theater without qualities, theater that needs only itself in order to define itself. Generally speaking, a people's theater as it is usually understood is the reflection of a fundamental disorder, that which consists in making dramatic art serve a purpose, in utilizing it in the service of political, civic or social beliefs. Or else, under the name "theater for the masses," it expresses another sort of deviation, through the spectacular displays it allows, the outpourings of collective enthusiasm for which it is a pretext, and which are used by the authorities to confirm the moral and national unity of a people. In the first case, we are in the presence of theater that has been deflected from its true course by a moralizing purpose or for propaganda purposes. In the second case, we witness the appearance of a theater of apotheosis that is governed most of the time by a political slogan, but that, when that is not the case, would still nevertheless be an instrument of artistic destruction, to the extent first of all that the effect it tends to create is one of crude excitability, which the state then uses for its own purposes, and second that in order to achieve these monstrous effects it inflicts on itself a profligacy of means that conflicts with the calculated stagecraft of dramatic art.

It is not difficult to see that even without being a response to such glaring excesses, the tendency nowadays to give encouragement to popular theater, or more generally to popular art, appears primarily as a dangerous temptation, aimed at luring the artist away from his essential vocation. It would seem that, on the pretext of becoming aware of the community, of reaching out to the public with whom he has in fact been far too concerned hitherto, the artist finds himself obliged out of duty to seek out the crudest and most artificial means in order to move either as many people as possible, or a popular audience, which is to say one that is without any culture whatsoever. There would seem furthermore to be an attempt to favor theater not because it is a higher form of artistic expression, but because by providing a feeling of human communion, it appears to be an unrivaled means of creating unity. Activities like these will found nothing durable and nothing profound. A dramatic work, like any work, arises out of solitude and is destined to plunge the man who comprehends it, in the very midst of the community of which he is conscious, into silence and into solitude. It comes from a solitary man and it returns to a solitary man. It creates silence at the heart of passion and it turns a brilliant celebration into an anxious, desolate quest. Pierre-Aimé Touchard is right to begin his remarkable *Apology for Theater* with these words taken from Paul Claudel, which express the profound vocation of dramatic art: "Let me be like the sower of solitude and let he who hears my words go back troubled to his home and heavy laden."[2]

—September 23, 1941

Mediterranean Inspirations

The book Jean Grenier has just published with the title *Mediterranean Inspirations* is a work that owes nothing to external events and would seem to have been set free from time.[1] Though it is made up of thoughts about those predestined sites where Western civilization took shape and looks to the traditional landscapes of our culture for wisdom that can be valid for everyone, it is marvelously indifferent to what in current circumstances could well lead many a mind to magnify such wisdom, and draw from it too precise a lesson that would be immediately tainted by the desire to make use of it and so rendered superfluous at the very moment it was applied. That lesson is a vital one. There is no reason to shackle wisdom, even in order to better appreciate what its value is. A man whose vocation has until now been to turn his gaze towards the pure elements of the present day, the vastest objects in his sphere of existence, has no reason now to turn back toward everyday life. Let him stay put inside that self in which his struggle is with conditions and contingencies. His specialty is a universal meditation that ceases to be of use as soon as its usefulness becomes apparent. As Jean Grenier writes: "These are troubled times? All times have been troubled times: the series of revolutions and wars is infinite. . . . Stendhal no longer means anything to us for his Russian campaign: he means everything to us for his *Charterhouse*. For us, Chateaubriand wasted his time as ambassador to the Pope; but we still have his reveries on the Roman countryside . . . what he called his wasted time."

Another of this book's merits is to be faithful to a genre that many works have made seem vaguer, less rule-bound, and more improvised than it ought to be: the genre of the essay. It is customary to include within this sort of writing any book that throws critical light on some vaguely general subject, and shows evidence of a degree of mental activity or of some haphazard effort at erudition. There are essays on the subject of everything: on Corneille, morality, style. Since everything is conventional, there is nothing to be said against this generalization of a term that promises nothing but its own modest ambition. It would seem nevertheless, if only because of the example provided by Montaigne, that the essay is above all the effort of a mind that goes from confidences to thoughts, from the concrete to the abstract, and that offers itself as an example in order to go beyond itself. The essay is an endeavor that is focused less on the subject it is concerned with, Corneille or style, than on the author who is in search of himself through writing it, and wants to discover himself there in the most general guise. It is an experience during which, sometimes indirectly, the writer does not only become involved, but opens himself up to dispute, presents himself as a problem, leads his ideas to a point where he is rejected by them, derives from his personal ordeals a meaning that is acceptable to everyone, in short, makes himself the hero of an adventure whose significance lies beyond him. In this respect there is a curious affinity between the essay and a certain type of novel. When we read novels in which the author says "I," we like to see them as an intellectual fiction that we attribute less to the writer than to a real person whom he creates almost from nothing. Indeed, certain minds eventually bring to light this actor whom they had initially ensconced inside the darkness of a theatre. Paul Valéry liked to say "I," but he also invented the character Leonardo da Vinci, then M. Teste, whose adventure he briefly recounted in a work that is, in some respects, the epitome of the *novel*.

What makes Jean Grenier's essay original is that it is concerned less with exploring Mediterranean wisdom and discovering or glorifying ancient civilizations, than with the effort of a mind that has deep affinities with their essential qualities yet cannot find its own equilibrium there. It is very precisely the story of an intellectual adventure. The mind it evokes finds within itself a love of the deep, a dizzying desire for the absolute. "The sea by whose shore I spent my childhood," he writes, "is not that sea with its sharply defined horizons we call the Mediterranean, but the endlessly changing and unstable ocean." He feels that this origin has left him with a certain liking for what is shapeless and undefined, a need for unstable dreams, a passion for indifference. His mind has been eroded. He can no longer create, he can only submit. In the total darkness through which he makes his way, he vainly tries to believe that everything is possible; and the absolute that tempts him leads simply to a destitution into which he blissfully sinks.

What is the Mediterranean for him? In the course of all the thoughts that Provence, the Roman countryside, evenings in Biskra, or Greek statues inspire in him, he puts together the rudiments of a wisdom that he unconsciously appropriates for himself, and with which he counters the disorder of his own ideas. He approaches those tombs on which we can still read inscriptions that give the dead perceptible form, link them to a generous humanity, and bear witness, from beyond extinction, to their survival. And he wonders: who drove them, at the moment when they left everything behind without illusions, to express their detachment? Who led those who loved art, but knew that art is perishable, to leave behind as a record a fine goblet, a fine statue, or a fine name? Was it an infantile urge to become immortal? Did they not know that whoever becomes famous dies twice, since glory is merely an extension of life that is as fleeting as life itself? Was it not rather a great feeling of compassion in man for man, "a fraternal wish to create, in the midst of a blazing, formless world, something which, held close to his heart, might give him the support of a *definition*"?

Such are the words that he hears by that sea, beneath that sun and that sky whose brilliance he can see and whose light allows the eye to consider all things without becoming lost in them. Wherever it reaches, Mediterranean wisdom *defines*. It obliges the mind to see possibilities as duties. It subjects the whole of nature to it, in its grandeur and its precision. It incorporates into landscapes and monuments an act of intelligence that turns every thing into the site of a revelation and a commemoration. In its essence, so it is said, Mediterranean language is that of Protagoras, who states that man is the measure of all things. There is no humdrum concern for anthropomorphism in this claim. The principal achievement of Mediterranean man lies in seeking within himself the point where he can compare himself with the world; where, having replaced the accidental, unstable, and fragmentary individual that he is with the universal self he carries within him, he bestows a generality upon himself that raises him to the power of the universe, allowing him to judge the plurality of what is singular, and free himself from chance. Thus does the notion of law take shape, providing a measure whereby consciousness stripped entirely of all personal attributes, reduced down to nothing but itself, laid waste and naked, rediscovers itself through a rediscovery of the world that it possesses, organizes, and contemplates. Know yourself, know yourself as a universal, as the point of reference for this universe, which, without you, is bottomless chaos.

The dialogue that Jean Grenier conducts with himself is perceptible only in certain inflections whose effects he carefully controls. It takes shape in the chapters that close the book, where the intellectual drama he is recalling appears more precisely. The mind whose twists and turns he reveals would appear to be torn between three attitudes or three temptations, corresponding to a cult of the absolute, a cult of action and a wisdom that lies equidistant between the one and the other. What has Mediterranean thought revealed to him? That people should desire what they possess, and wish with all their might the fate that is allotted to them. But someone who is intoxicated with the absolute finds it impossible to give up the desire that drives him, in its excessive purity, through a labyrinth of ice toward an incorruptible unity. He seeks to become one with a God he cannot find, and able neither to create himself nor to attach himself to a creator, all that remains for him is to collapse into indifference and be either damned or saved by a blindly gratuitous act, the expression of a will to live that spurns all justification.

This is an eternal dialogue. Jean Grenier does not renew its terms or go deeper into its significance. In a pure and gentle language, he contemplates in melancholic fashion the uncertainties in the midst of which his mind flounders, and that he attempts to bring to an end through the precision of his analyses and the honesty of his language. Does this silent adventure have an outcome? In art, perhaps, which brings will and action, action and the absolute into harmony, and transforms shapeless fate into personal destiny. "When you look at the mute faces of Greek statues," he writes, "you can see them smile, from the kouroi and korai of the archipelago to the figures of Alexandria." What is the meaning of this smile? It is a timid appeal, an uncertain dawn, a barely acknowledged hope. It invites man to work within the world as if the world were of importance, while persuading him that it has none. And it invites him to love glory, while alerting him to the fact that to love glory is to seek to make imperishable what he knows in advance must be vanquished. Such is wisdom: a joy that is inseparable from truth.

Around this brief work there plays a hum of reverie, a murmur of melancholy and tender despair, a sort of absence at the heart of attention that seemingly gives it its entire value. Whatever the quality of the reflections it calls forth, it is sustained above all by a certain turn of mind, by the internal images to be found therein, and by a gentle incline that is also a lazy drift through ups and downs and through anxieties. On the subject of Mediterranean wisdom we have other books, *Anthinea* in particular, and that book is all we need.[2] But by tracing with such skill and purity the misfortunes of a mind that has been tempted by the abyss, and is slowly reborn as it contemplates the circumstances that surround civilization, Jean Grenier offers a personal account whose significance is not limited to the ideas it raises. One hears in it the voice that language brings to thought when the latter, aware of its impotence, asks words to provide a veiled consolation that renders it bitter and secret.

—September 30, 1941

Unknown or Underrated Authors

The book that Valéry Larbaud has recently devoted to a selection of French authors of his choosing, *French Domain*, is full of grace and affection.[1] Anyone who did not yet know this diffident writer, and who tried to discover him in this book where he speaks of the poets and novelists he likes, would have the pleasure of seeking him in elegant discussion, a language of nuance and a delicacy of passion that conceals itself behind a sort of decorum of expression. The modesty of the form he is content with entails a liking for muted colors designed to deceive its reader's gaze. Those who read like to be provoked. What Valéry Larbaud has to offer is not easy, but neither is it difficult. He attracts readers neither with the pleasure of being entertained, nor with the profundity of an enigma. He creates for himself a solitude within an invisible perfection.

It would be easy to consider his book as the expression of an erudite mind with a love of letters, attaching itself to them obligingly and serenely, and taking a dilettante's pleasure in the discoveries they offer and in the skillful advocacy for which they provide an opportunity. Could there be a more diverse set of writers than those with whom he displays an affinity? There is an almost jarring variety in the art of Maurice Scève, that of Lingendes or the celebrated vulgarities of Dondey de Santeny. How can a mind display the same eagerness when extending momentary favor to authors whom everything separates, except for a common experience of wounded glory? Can he be the friend of writers who seem to cancel each other out? Where is the balance in such complacent judgment?

It would no doubt be easy to see behind Valéry Larbaud's choices no other rule than one dictated by tastes that are too broad, and to accuse him of a lack of discrimination. That is the sort of reproach that authors of anthologies attract and sometimes deserve, and in *French Domain* there is what amounts to a plan for an anthology of French prose and poetry in which authors would be chosen less for their merits than for the degree of injustice inflicted on them by posterity. That is indeed one of Valéry Larbaud's concerns, it would appear. Most of the writers he is drawn to have not survived the reputation they acquired during their lives, or have even failed to be anything other than obscure: Antoine Héroët, Jean de Lingendes, or Dondey de Santeny, for example. Others, such as Maurice Scève, thanks in particular to Valéry Larbaud it should be said, but also in part thanks to the efforts of Joseph Aynard, are gradually being restored to the place of honor in French literature that they deserve. But the long eclipse into which the admirable art of Scève, one of the foremost representatives of French poetic art, disappeared for several centuries, has given this posthumous favor a proud and intimate character that makes it very different from a clear-cut case of fame. In Valéry Larbaud's book we find the elements of a strange argument concerning the injustices of fate and the vicissitudes of posterity. Boileau, as we know, appealed to posterity as the only infallible judge and only irrefutable critic: "Whatever the impact a writer may have had during his life, however much praise he may have received, it cannot be claimed infallibly on those counts that his works are excellent.

. . . Only the approval of posterity can establish the true merit of a work."[2] That is a strange, even incredible thought, whose true meaning would seem to have been much neglected. How can we ignore the fact that posterity is made up of the same haphazardness, the same eccentricity, and the same complacency as public opinion? Ever lazy, ever a prey to the habits and foibles of judgment, it represents merely the uncertainties of the public mind, not to mention the material circumstances that threaten reputations as well as works and place the value of what is written at the mercy of a physical accident. It is certainly excessive to make the merits of a work depend on that great and absurd system of suffrage we call posterity. Through his concern to evaluate works in terms of their spiritual fecundity, Boileau was probably conveying the intemporal character that he attributed to perfect works. It was not a matter of removing them from time. Works do not have value because of the long series of men who judge them; they are a constant response, which is sometimes admired, sometimes neglected, often entirely unrecognized, to the questions and the myths that make up time.

By attaching himself with his precise and cordial judgment to a number of unrecognized figures in our literature, Valéry Larbaud has nevertheless made room for several writers, like Prosper Mérimée or Paul Valéry, who by making brilliant names for themselves created a precise echo of their creations. But it is in the very coincidence that brings together the forgotten and rightly forgotten name of Dondey de Santeny and the brilliant and justly brilliant name of Paul Valéry, that one of the justifications for *French Domain* probably lies. It would seem that Larbaud has sought out not only writers who were without fame or whom fame betrayed, but also those writers who sought rather to betray fame by rejecting its conditions. The one or two historically very valuable pages he devotes to the author of *The Young Fate* are designed primarily to shed some light on the withdrawal that the latter imposed on himself for eighteen years, and that only an accident of friendship prevented from being definitive.³ Those years of silence, that vow of abstinence, that refusal to be a writer, constitute one of the most important phenomena in the history of artistic creation. Its significance is no doubt manifold, and this is not the place to try and establish what it is. All that can be brought out is the nature of that solitude that is not only necessary for the artist but will also endure until it has consumed him, devoured him, and caused him to perish from a pitiless passion for a perfection he can never attain. The most authentic writer, as Mallarmé was wont to claim, is thus one who dreams with precision before a blank page, and who refuses to appear in order to be, detached from all illusions and from the monstrous complacency that is reflected in even the most rigorous and self-aware works.

In this respect, the history of Dondey de Santeny also merits a degree of attention. Having given him back his real name (under the pseudonym Philothée O'Neddy, Dondey is the author of a collection of poems entitled *Fire and Flame*, which appeared in 1833 and was reissued in 1926), and defended Dondey's somewhat feeble qualities with his usual taste, Valéry Larbaud recalls his miserable career.⁴ Though very aware of his solemn vocation, this poet, who alongside Petrus Borel played a small part in the Jeune France movement during the second Romantic period, rapidly withdrew into silence, and yielding more to a taste for artistic asceticism than to any good reasons for discouragement there might be, he gave up all thought of poetry for ten years. After that period, he turned his hand once again to the art of writing, but without seeking to have his writings published. Valéry Larbaud is loyal in his praise of the works of this period, and of one poem in particular: "The Cripple," "thirty-four verses of six alexandrines each, with two rhymes which are alternating and consecutive by turns, and with a breadth and solidity that recall the most famous poems of Romanticism."⁵ Despite his qualities, Dondey nevertheless remained unknown, isolated, and unhappy, working against his will, tempted at every instant to give up once and for all, and yet embarked upon a great cosmic poem that combined certain memories of Maurice Scève's *Microcosm* and certain inklings of Mallarmean technique with a number of almost excruciating vulgarities and idiocies.[6] Such is this artist who managed to avoid fame while at the same time having nothing to withhold from it. He represents the final episode in the drama of posterity that Valéry Larbaud describes, and in which, alongside admirable authors who were once unappreciated and have now been brought back to light such as Maurice Scève, and alongside writers who tried unsuccessfully to outwit their fate through remaining silent such as Paul Valéry, he draws attention to a touchingly mediocre poet who found in the willing self-effacement of withdrawal the true oblivion he both foresaw and perhaps desired.

The case of Jean de Lingendes, another of those writers whom anthologies leave out, reflects a quite different whim of fame. This poet, the most charming of whose verse Valéry Larbaud reminds us of, was very widely known in his time. Boileau had no hesitation in speaking of him in the same breath as Malherbe and Racan, naturally placing him well above Ronsard and du Bellay. For a century and a half, such popularity proved stronger than neglect or discredit, but then it gradually became dormant, and the oblivion that has overtaken Lingendes today seems like a sign of indifference or exhausted attention that no good reason appears to justify. Valéry Larbaud rightly claims for him a place alongside poets such as Étienne Durand, François Maynard, and Tristan l'Hermite, and the following lines, taken from the "Ode on the Queen's Mourning," which he quotes "as displaying a quality that is unique in all of French poetry," would certainly have a claim to immortality, if immortality had any meaning for a work of art:

> And after, surrounded in great veils,
> The sad and pious garb

Of that fine head for which stars
Would be a more fitting adornment,
You would resemble that chariot
Which, hiding its light by day
Only shines in the evening,
When during the more funereal nights,
Entirely attired in shadow,
She dares not show her face.[7]

On putting down *French Domain*, one is no longer in any
doubt as to the unity that governs its development, or the
reasons behind a choice that appears so difficult to comprehend. From Maurice Scève to Mérimée, from Mérimée to
Charles-Louis Philippe and León-Paul Fargue, one is consis-
tently confronted with artists who are either obscure or else
have been obscured, and who are so discreet, so subtly harmo-
nious that as a result even when their reputations seem
unshakable, they risk falling victim to silent, calm obliteration.
That discretion and that silence are a precise expression of
Valéry Larbaud's own profound art. It is impossible to over-
state the merits of the gentle patience, aloof reserve, and precise, distinct politeness with which he pursues his thinking
and invites his reader to take part. Some of his studies are
based on great learning and show evidence of a highly elaborate critical apparatus. But he avoids giving any air of great
learning to these discussions about a word or a historical con-
jecture, or to the minutiae that he surrounds with notes, and
he seems to want to show his ignorance at the very moment
he reveals the utter perfection of his labor. Finally, in this
criticism without vanity there is such a fervent respect for art
that despite the author's discretion, one looks in it for the
mirror in which he sees himself, reveals himself, and offers
himself to himself. This is the sort of confidence that reveals a
secret by hiding it more thoroughly. Take, for example, what
Valéry Larbaud himself writes about Mérimée: "Mérimée does
not have an immediate effect on the mind of the reader. The
effect begins only once reading is over. He has sketched out

the attitudes of his characters baldly, almost meagerly, and given a very rapid account of what they have done; then he has whisked them away, more often than not killed them, eliminated them. . . . But that is when they start to live." That is precisely what one is inclined to say of Valéry Larbaud and his writings, which are so exquisite, so restrained, and so expressive.

—October 14, 1941

Terror in Literature

The book that Jean Paulhan has just devoted to literature and language gives rise to strange feelings in its reader. You follow the arguments he develops without a second thought, and with no sense of the perils toward which you are being driven by his precise and delightful sentences, whose tight construction offers a guarantee of safety and order. Everything here is clear, ingenious, and straightforward. Just as the words follow on from each other without disruption, so there emerges a succession of solid reasons whose main purpose seems above all to be to dispel uncertainty and guarantee the basic method of any writer. We calmly look on as a certain notion of criticism is disabled, seemingly with no regrets for its defeat, since its tendencies made it hostile to customs and rules. And yet an initial feeling of anxiety creeps in. While remaining marvelously cogent and regular, the movement of thought that we are trying to follow is accompanied by digressions and allusions whose meaning is ominous. Where is this author going? He seemed just to be doing a little humdrum police work with exquisite talent. Is he not talking about something different from what we assumed? Could there be, hidden inside his refutations and his arguments, a sort of time bomb that, though invisible today, will one day explode, and so devastate literature that it will become unfit for use? Such is the anxiety that Jean Paulhan can provoke. You read his book unwarily, but when you reach its close you suddenly see that he has called into question not only a certain notion of criticism, not only all of literature, but also the mind, its powers and its means, and you look back with horror at the abyss over which you have just walked—but have you really crossed it?—and that remained skillfully veiled from view as you went over it. Jean Paulhan has given two titles to his work, *The Flowers of Tarbes* and *Terror in Literature*, and this ambiguity anticipates one or two of the tricks that he uses in order to manipulate our minds.[1]

When asked the question "What is literature?" the criticism that Jean Paulhan calls "terrorist" gives the following answer: literature is to be found only where there are no clichés, only when a poem or a novel does not cloak itself in conventions, contrivances, or predictable figures. This terror, whose decrees have governed literature for the last hundred and fifty years, is the expression of a need for purity, a desire to break with everything that even extends to forgetting the common conditions of language. With Victor Hugo it rejects "rhetoric," with Verlaine "eloquence," with Rimbaud "poetic old hat"; but with more recent writers, driven by an aversion to cliché and tormented by the feeling that they ought to revolt, it purports to break with all forms of discourse and even all language, seeking in originality a temporary refuge for a rebellion that is constantly drained of energy by its own success. Loss of words, poverty of vocabulary, but also an absolute suspicion of technique, well-defined genres and rules more generally: such are the effects of Terror, which, from Sainte-Beuve to Taine, from Romanticism to Surrealism, encloses literature inside a network of defenses where it can only flourish. At the entrance to the municipal park in Tarbes, says Jean Paulhan, this notice can be seen: "It is forbidden to enter the park carrying flowers." The same notice can also be found nowadays at the entrance to literature. There young writers can show themselves only if their hands are pure, and if they lack those ornaments with which art was naturally embellished in former times, and so appear with all the brilliance and disorder of a freedom that is vainly striving to go back to the wild.

Why such a fear of commonplace? Because, says terrorist criticism, cliché is a place of laziness and inertia. A writer who comes to rest there complacently indulges an indolence that subjects him to ready-made forms. He continues to believe that he is thinking for himself; but he is mistaken: he is accepting a succession of words that imposes an established order on him and seals off his thinking tightly. The use of commonplace thus leads to the serious abuse we call verbalism. A prey to conventional sentences, the author is no longer the master of his words, and words, triumphing over the precise meaning to which they ought to correspond, recalcitrant toward the mind that seeks to guide them, press down on him with their brutal weight, making him feel all of its degrading supremacy. If one thinks of words such as liberty, democracy, or order, and of the chaos that can result if they are used indiscriminately, then it is clear that writers are justified in being vigilant in order that such facile enslavement may be prevented. Though they appear to have surrendered to license and anarchy, in fact they are engaged in the task of rejecting chance, obscurity, and confusion, in smashing idols and in fighting monsters.

In other words, Terror, the enemy of commonplace and rules, is a struggle against a sickness of language, and fearing that words, left to themselves and independently of what they mean, will wield daunting power over the hearts and minds of men, it seeks to give unlimited influence to inspiration and creative force. Jean Paulhan notes that this notion of terror encountered in Bergson's philosophy a doctrine that was perfectly designed to allow it to achieve self-awareness. Which is to say, following Bergson's advice, it invited the writer to work unceasingly against the language of practical life so as to redis-cover the fluid forms of a deeper life. Beyond surface logic, which is made rigid by everyday words, it goes in search of a reality that is unexpressed and probably inexpressible; it seeks to break through the network of convention in order to reach a world that is still innocent; it lays claim to a virgin contact, to fresh new meanings, and finds in its aspiration toward extreme purity a justification for the imperious decrees that allow it to cast suspicion on the expertise and technique that are designed for common use.

Such is Terror; such are its pretensions, its hates, and its secrets. What should we think of it? If its grievances are exam-ined with a little care, it is clear first of all that they do not correspond to even the simplest observation; and second, that they are based on an illusion of a remarkable kind. For it would be unwise to believe that the use of commonplace always presupposes laziness or encourages verbalism. There are cases where the writer invents his clichés, rediscovering them through personal effort and using them as a means of express-ing freshness of feeling or candor of imagination. There are cases where the author knows he is using commonplace but uses it willingly, precisely because for him it simply represents a form of language that is as usual as any other word, perfectly adapted to its meaning and incapable of obscuring it. Clichés are designed to go unnoticed, and far from making the sen-tences that include them appear verbally excessive, their effect is rather to make them transparent and invisible by virtue of their very banality.

In reality, the accusations of Terror are based entirely on an optical illusion. Its gaze is directed at the author, whom it accuses of yielding to words, when in fact it is the reader, grappling with commonplace, who is entirely preoccupied with words, and the prisoner of an unclear language whose intention escapes him. When the writer uses a cliché, the per-son who reads him can ask himself at least two questions: is that, he asks, a picturesque and empty expression that translates and brings out an important idea, or is it on the contrary a grand utterance to which nothing corresponds? It is this ambiguity that mars the use of conventional words and makes it dangerous. The reader, embarrassed and uneasy, wondering what can possibly be the meaning of words like liberty, order, or democracy that people use in his presence, ends up accusing the author of verbalism, as if he were guilty of having neglected these words, and rather than being too interested in the combinations of language, being insufficiently attentive to problems of form, whose solution he leaves to his reader, so that it is he who is henceforth given over entirely to words and possessed by them.

The flaw in commonplace, in cliché, or in a familiar succession of images is thus that they plunge whoever reads them into ambiguity, and distance him from the thought to which he ought to gain access. In that light, it is clear how the attitude that accuses rhetoric is right to urge the writer to search for a faithful expression, and why it is justified in denouncing the scandal of commonplace that, instead of faultlessly fulfilling its role as a scrupulous interpreter, on the contrary encourages obscurity and misunderstanding. But it is also clear that this interpretation is incomplete. Terror, so intransigent, so swift to pounce on a figure, is in fact extraordinarily timid. It is content to act after the error has been committed, pursuing clichés when they have already done their work of corruption, and lashing out at random with no clear concern for the reasons behind the justice it metes out. Terror thus needs to be improved upon, and the best way of making it into a means of preventive action, which is to say of dispelling the two-faced form that is that of the commonplace, is to deprive the latter of the power to cheat that it possesses, to make its character one of luminous self-evidence, in short to make commonplace *common*, whereas its principal flaw, according to the preceding remarks, was to be an expression that constantly wavers, that is not fixed or commonly understood. And the same goes for other conventions, rules, laws, and figures. The writer who makes use of them correctly, who is prepared to forge them through the power of a flawless technique, and not to submit to them, is rewarded with an innocent literature and a language closely allied to things. Rhetoric or perfect Terror, as Jean Paulhan puts it.

It would be most regrettable to read *The Flowers of Tarbes* without seeing the multiple meanings behind the thinking that expresses itself there, and whose murmur, along with a number of lightning reversals or on the contrary one or two slow allusions, gives a hint of its enigmatic existence. We should not believe that this book is what it seems to be: an examination by the most subtle, rare and felicitous of minds into a specific critical notion, and a proposal for an ingenious solution to a particular problem. In fact, it raises a fundamental question concerning the nature of the mind, its profound division, the combat between same and same that is the source of its power, its torment, and its apotheosis. Whoever attempts to read the true book that Jean Paulhan has written, and whose sequel we are promised, will find that beneath the ironical reserve for which he has the gift, by means of a seriousness that contests itself and tests itself in the process, he has posed in a form that recalls Kant's celebrated revolution the following problem: How is literature possible? But since a question like that, through the debate into which it draws language and the mind, implies a hypothesis concerning the nature of our utmost darkness, we may at least glimpse some of the pathways that it follows in order to reach a level of authentic thought and contemplate its native purity, which is itself made up of stereotypes, commonplace, and conventions. These thoughts cannot be expressed in a few words. We hope to have the opportunity, in another study, to set out the reasons that make this book one of the most important works of contemporary critical writing.[2]

—October 21, 1941

The Writer and the Public

It would be possible to take a rather dim view of the little book that J.-N. Faure-Biguet has just written about *Montherlant's Childhoods*.[1] The very idea, some may say: to devote so many pages to the vagaries of youth in a writer who has only just left youth behind; to recall in painstaking detail the writings of a nine-year-old child, when the reader already has enough to deal with in the works of the grown man; to focus all attention on a life at its beginnings, as if the work that follows made everything important, even things that in no way pre-suppose its existence—what a perfectly vain, thankless, and unpleasant task! All these things can indeed be said. Those who read are all too inclined to read an author because they know one or two details about his life and are taken with that life. The work is almost forgotten about. It is a mere pretext, and it vanishes as soon as it has provided the handful of auto-biographical elements expected of it. Art that has no truck with intimate secrets becomes a means of daydreaming about its author.

Faure-Biguet is thus not totally innocent when, despite his concern to eliminate all unnecessary anecdote, he implies that we would know Montherlant's work better if we knew more about the person who wrote it. That is probably an error in the case of most writers, but it is definitely wrong for a writer who appears to have made himself the subject of almost all his books, and been so constantly preoccupied with himself that he seems to be present in everything he writes. Let one thing be clear: the author is never the man. Falsifications and compromises always enter into things, and these constitute the indispensable contribution of art. The artist is powerless not to feel the wish to create a finished work, in which his own figure and his own existence are modified so as to fit the form that will render them essential. As there are perhaps only nuances separating autobiographical truth from the expression given to it by the work in which it is recorded, the reader who wishes to discover it is tempted to ignore those nuances, though they alone constitute the effects of art, or to consider them basely as specious lies that he can then challenge. He foolishly reproaches the writer with being a writer. He is angry with him because he has discovered something the writer did not tell him, or else told him about in a way that conflicts with what the facts seemed to dictate. He demands that the mirror be broken. He rejects the sole image worthy of the attention of his gaze.

And yet if Faure-Biguet has been unable to avoid all the pitfalls of his subject, he can be praised for explaining why he decided to risk them. The story that matters in the case of any artist is not the story of his life but the story of his pride. How did he resist what was futile in his nature, his initial wish to please, the urge to be seen and admired, the pleasure of meaning something to others, the abominable urge to be the creature of public opinion? By what efforts did he gradually take himself in hand, find glory in ignoring the public, refuse to beguile people's minds and be as content to be himself in opposition to others as he initially was to disguise himself a little, and to lie to himself on others' behalf? And last, casting his nets ever higher to use Paul Valéry's expression, and having first obligingly made himself too similar to the public, then defiantly too dissimilar to it, in what state of solitude did he abandon this as yet still external manifestation of himself, and taking the route of simplest feeling, at last discover a pure image of his true being? These questions concerning the artist are relevant to art because they follow one of the paths of artistic creation. Faure-Biguet cannot be blamed for having alluded to them in the case of a writer who has constantly offered the spectacle of a soul troubled by the ambitions of its pride.

There is in Henri de Montherlant an awareness of what he is as a writer, and more generally of what the correct relations are between the work and the person who created it, which is of the greatest relevance today. Faure-Biguet tells us that from a very early age, Montherlant was driven by a prodigious love of writing. By the time he was about ten, he had not only covered reams of paper with scribble and written short stories, novels, and historical tales, he had also compiled a comprehensive bibliography of his own works and employed one or two tricks of the author's trade out of a curious desire for publicity. If such youthful quirks have any meaning, it is because they show how intimately a pure love of literature and a rare appetite for fame and the glamorous life coexisted in a mind that was so clearly destined for the highest literary honors. What is more, other episodes from his youth, such as his time at the Collège Sainte-Croix, show that his early instincts were combined with others that were no less violent, such as the urge to exert an influence or power of spiritual guidance, to be an awakener, to cause surprise, to lead others by means of a wholly inward superiority and a proud and demanding outward expression of himself. At Sainte-Croix he became the president of a literary *académie*, and with some friends he founded a sort of order whose dimensions soon become a cause of scandal in the eyes of those in charge of the institution. Henri de Montherlant was expelled.

These three passions are enough to hint at the strange debates to which they can give rise in the soul of a man who, as one predestined to be a writer, thinks only of himself, but who remembers too, with an eye on his fame, that he is in the public eye, and out of a superior affinity for power and perhaps devotion is determined to speak for others and have an effect upon them. In Montherlant we witness an extraordinary consolidation of those instincts, although none of them will consent to nullify itself and disappear entirely; sometimes one of them will summon him back with extreme force to the purity of his own self and its irreducible strangeness; sometimes another will drive him to take account of the effects of that self on strangers whose attention he draws to it; sometimes a third will provoke him to come out of himself through a desire to charm and to communicate. It is unceasingly a struggle and a clash in which the various beings a writer may carry inside him confront each other. All he wants is to be increasingly himself, but the three men he is pitted against are also him after a fashion, and they variously urge him to put himself to work, give himself some scope, or else fall back, depending on the force they encounter in the combined resources of his vanity and his pride.

There is no question with Montherlant of following the direction and the movement of this profound dialectic, which has led him to the fierce and jealous delight of being himself, and also to the need to bear witness to his solitude, and present to the public the hidden and ingenuous solitary being whose precious treasure he defends. What we should not forget is that this twofold and threefold passion has allowed him to define precisely the relations between the writer and public affairs. In this essential, Montherlant has never wavered. Be it in *The Young Infanta of Castille*, during the crisis of *the Hunted Travellers* in 1927, in 1934 in the texts that make up *Useless Service* or in the pages that appeared in the *Nouvelle Revue française* in September 1941 on the subject of the freedom of the mind, he repeatedly asserts the fundamental truth that a writer should have only one concern: to express entirely his inner core, to make everything secondary to that expression, and if necessary, to sacrifice everything to it.[2] It could be said that this is merely stating the obvious; but as Montherlant in his turn calmly puts it after Goethe: "It is not a matter of saying new things, but of saying again and again what has already been said." It therefore bears repeating today that a writer worthy of the name is strictly speaking under no obligation whatsoever to take account of the public; that it is enough for him to be loyal with himself, and that this loyalty consists first and foremost in focusing entirely on his work, and being faithful to the necessity of that work which is one that no one but he can write, and on which he depends through an inner destiny; and then that this loyalty should lead him to discount all questions that do not form part of his inner core, and above all, to refrain from offering peremptory and categorical opinions on these questions. As compensation, the public should allow the writer to act according to his particular inclinations, leaving him with the responsibility for his destiny and only judging him by his ultimate work.

Montherlant adds quite rightly that these remarks are valid in normal times, but at a time when circumstances seem to impose on everyone an additional duty of service, it is the writer's duty to limit his involvement with that service to that of a man who shoulders his rucksack when the alert sounds, in the knowledge that his destiny lies elsewhere. "The public should remember," he writes, "that a great writer serves his country through his work more, much much more, than through the action he may involve himself in, and that it is an error of judgment to ask a man to work in shifting sands when if he is simply left to get on, he will work in bronze." It naturally goes without saying that writers whose work is essentially political in nature are justified in defending it for what it is; but with others, one can merely recall the words of Goethe to Fritz von Müller: "Whoever wants to do something for the world should have nothing to do with it," or this remark made to Eckermann: "Whoever does not withdraw entirely from this din and force himself to remain in isolation is lost."

It is clearly necessary to draw attention to these words and fiercely defend their meaning and their force. There is much talk today of art, the public and how important it is for the creator to stay in close touch with the person for whom he creates. It must be said that this makes no sense whatever, other than to reveal the extraordinary mediocrity of people who discuss serious problems without knowing what they are talking about. Absolutely nothing can be said, and nothing asked of a creator from without. His ways are unknown. It is often through a supremely inhuman effort, a meticulous search for what is unalike in him, a demented instinct for pride and solitude that he brings to light that store of human excellence whose riches are inestimable. Everything that could make him deviate from his nature, his indifference, and a self that is extraordinarily alien to all the rest; everything that, on whatever pretext, whether it be service to society or service to the nation, a desire for devotion or an act of sympathy, lures him away from his unapproachable inner island so as to impose on him some current concern or some thought for the public, inflicts a wound on him from which he may well never recover. That has been true in every age and of every creator. The best-intentioned advice given to an artist is either ridiculous or execrable. Every single time such questions come to mind, the story of Filippo Lippi should be invoked, for it contains all there is to say on the subject. "While working for the Medicis," says Montherlant, "the painter Filippo Lippi had to be locked up because he loved life so much; but he managed to escape through a window. In the end, Cosimo said: 'Leave the door open for him. Men of talent are heavenly creatures. They must not be constrained in any way.'"[3]

—November 4, 1941

Huysmans's Secret

It may well be that Huysmans's memory has survived more because of the interest that his conversion still arouses than owing to any curiosity about his works. And even in those works of his that are still read, such as *The Cathedral,* there is no certainty that what people are seeking is simple literary pleasure rather than grounds for moral improvement or devotion.[1] The readers who prolong and preserve the reputation of a writer are quite often those whom the writer would have vehemently hated and despised. The artist continues to exist with the aid of what he would gladly have suppressed. Nonetheless, Huysmans's fame raises issues that are important not just for literary history, but for literature considered as something living and durable. It is enough to think of the Naturalist school and the authors who accepted its rules, to recognize by contrast the authenticity and value of the art that reveals that school's limitations. If Huysmans's life still holds our attention so entirely, it is because it expressed in an immediately visible form the principles and powers of renewal from which his work also benefited.

In two short books that have come out together, one by
Lucien Descaves (*The Last Years of J.-K. Huysmans*) and one
by Maurice Garçon (*The Unknown Huysmans*), we encounter
the memory of a life that was already quite transformed by
spiritual preoccupations, a life that was tormented and mysterious, anxious and difficult, more ardent and spontaneous
than ever in the midst of its purification.[2] Both books are
admirably discreet. What they keep silent about is more
important than what they are willing to say. Maurice Garçon,
who has many links with Ligugé, deals in particular with
Huysmans's stay close by the abbey and the vows he took
there. Lucien Descaves, who was his friend, host, and literary
executor, follows the writer until his death. Everything he
writes about the secret ordeals that filled Huysmans's last years
is characterized by a spirit of prudence, a concern for respect
and for truth, which successfully gives the lie to many other
accounts, where what can scarcely be revealed is inconsider-
ately discussed.

What is striking about Huysmans's religious life, at least
seen from the outside, is the great impatience it reveals, an
irritability that sustains an extreme concern for freedom even
within obedience itself. Chance and feeling at its most authentic constantly worked together to bring the author of *En route*
to a resolute decision.[3] It is not clear whether he is the play-
thing or the master of circumstance. If he comes to Ligugé, it
is at the insistence of a friend whom initially he simply wishes
to visit. Then he discovers a piece of land in a suitable location, which he reluctantly buys during negotiations in which
he comes off worse. Once the deal is done, he explodes in a
temper: "I've been diddled," he says to a friend. "This is
completely crazy. What a darned stupid idea it was to come
to this area where there are only clerics and boring business-
men!" It is on those terms that he consents to a choice that
will determine his spiritual destiny and confirm his vocation
as a Benedictine lay brother. At the same time, he appears to
devote all his energies to a struggle with insignificant problems

out of which he constructs for himself a formidable world. Lucien Descaves and Maurice Garçon both describe the lengths to which he goes in order to oblige an annoying old woman to keep her distance, and his torments when he does not succeed. They also depict the harassment and concern he feels when all of his books have to be moved elsewhere, or at the petty material arrangements in his life. On his return from Ligugé, the expulsion of the Congregations having forced him to return to Paris, the problem of finding a house where he would not be plagued by the minor discomforts of life became an obsession. Staying with the Benedictines of the rue Monsieur, where he has no freedom and few amenities, he tragically writes: "I can't go on! I want to escape, but what can I do?" Moving to the rue de Babylone for a while, he is consumed with impatience because during the night he hears the sound of milkmen and during the day a wretched duo playing the flute and the piano. He goes off to live in the rue Saint-Placide, worried this time that his rent is going to rise beyond a level he can afford. Everything is a cause of loathing and fatigue, and a reason to condemn his unbearable life.

Such excessive grumbling about perfectly natural discomforts would be of little significance were it not accompanied by a silence that seems to become ever greater as more and more trying problems bear down on him. Lucien Descaves has alluded to some of these sufferings, which were purely personal and which Huysmans was reluctant to divulge: anxieties about the mystical life to which he felt drawn without being able to endure its demands ("My soul is absolutely shattered," he wrote after a stay at La Trappe); confusion at having to abandon his project for a convent of Christian artists at Ligugé; profound anguish when he abandons occultist practices and leaves behind a penchant for magic spells in favor of a truer knowledge of the immense darkness ("Since my return to Paris," he writes, "it has started up again worse than ever, and all day yesterday and last night I was in agony"); a crisis of conscience that tormented him until the end of his life; and finally, horrible physical suffering: he lost his sight for several months, was operated on for an incurable cancer, and became agonizingly aware of his own death. Concerning the ordeals that entirely occupied his last years, his private diary contains only a single reference: "1905. End of shingles. Seven months blind. 1906. Operation. Three dreadful Christmases. Via dolorosa."

This silence regarding matters of importance, which goes together with a certain lack of restraint when complaining about trivial ones, offers a curious way of reacting to the world that is quite typical of Huysmans. Anxious by temperament, as a good Naturalist he has a veritable horror of reality, and this aversion is taken to such an extreme and affects him so violently that he seems endowed with a real genius for searching out what will offend or shock him. He seems to be perpetually on the lookout, contemplating with eager disgust and injured curiosity the countless horrors and abominations of existence. He has a nose for what he cannot abide, and goes looking for things he then wishes he had not found. He sees what is disgusting and horrible before anyone else, and wherever he does not encounter it, he creates it himself in order to be able to suffer from it, complain about it, and describe it. But that is just the first step. Prone to imagine in detail the visible misfortunes that offend him, he also focuses on more hidden levels of depravity, on excesses whose location is invisible, and whose peculiarity attracts him, repels him, and satisfies him. He becomes no less fond of outlandish superstition than he was curious about the scandalous side of contemporary life. He relishes the sordid ventures of bogus necromancers just as much as the wretched schemes of the stupid and the ugly. Stories of witchcraft terrify him, and he cannot do without them. He flees what is strange, and what is strange has such a strong grip on him that instead of continuing with a game that is exciting within its own limits, he devotes his life deeply and completely to the mystery around which up until then it had danced with impunity.

Such an outcome reveals what enigmatic consequences a certain literary outlook on the world, a certain purely artistic disdain for things and a search for what is bizarre that is governed by stylistic concerns can eventually bring about in a writer's existence. Huysmans, whose unfamiliar and excessive art regularly offended Catholic readers, was in effect saved by that need for what is exceptional whose palpable intensity is reflected in his language. While distaste sent him in pursuit of a reality that he rejected, he was able simultaneously to keep his sensibility intact and his heart pure for a world that would be more authentic and profound, and to go on being that highly strung individual, extreme in his judgments and fascinated by what is harsh and hateful, who sometimes took the passing observer by surprise. Though he talked at length about his conversion, and though his books are merely reflections of his own moods, it is fair to say that he defended the true nature of his inner secret against prying eyes, keeping the strange face he did not want to reveal well hidden, and though he would readily rebel for the least thing, keeping to himself the unbearable ordeals that brought both gloom and light into his life. It appears too that a modicum of humor (something other Naturalists were far from sharing) allowed him to avoid the consequences to which his pursuit of faults and follies could have led. The imagination still has its place in the realm of triviality and ugliness where he seems to thrive. He has a playful relation with himself, and makes no secret of the fact. If he is indignant, he defuses his anger by making it excessive in a comic episode where it appears exaggerated, and then he calms himself down by retreating into himself, without having committed his entire mental life to observing the ills that he denounces.

This same humor would seem to have enriched his style with one or two special qualities. We know what his language was like at the time when he was obliged to go one better than the Goncourts, and endow artistic writing with a surfeit of artifice: an effort at producing well-wrought images, taking expressions to an extreme, extracting a sense of refinement from trivial forms, forcing words into unexpected encounters, and subjecting syntax to difficult transpositions and irregularities. Such concern for literary craft, which so easily becomes outdated and can rapidly appear futile, was successfully corrected by an irony that kept its pedantic tendencies at bay. Sometimes, in a parody of style, this language appears spontaneous thanks to the rhythm of its deformations and the solidity of its unlikely couplings. Since it cannot possibly be accused of mannerism, it gives the impression that its true purpose lies in subjecting itself to derision, and making its use of rare terms and peculiar coinages appear less solemn. It is redeemed by the ambiguous nature of its contrivances. It takes itself purely for what it is, an unstable moment in an arbitrary and provisional construct of literary language. Huysmans thus presents an image of a rather mysterious and difficult art, but less because of his methods than owing to the ambivalent form taken by his intentions. What was simple and authentic about his life was never revealed, so that what appeared was merely the surface wrangling of a nervous, irritable, and credulous soul. In the same way his works, which are surprising rather than substantial, overloaded rather than truly rich, contain within them the potential for a parodic, hidden art that, had it been fully developed, would have left a decisive mark on literature.

—November 18, 1941

The Man in a Hurry

Paul Morand has just published a book that would be a real pleasure to read, were it not for the suspicion that we are expected while reading it to look for symbolic allusions, a deeper purpose, or else hidden motives whose subtle workings refuse to be pinned down. What precisely was his aim in writing the novel he has called *The Man in a Hurry*?[1] It is impossible to say. No doubt he wished first and foremost to organize the most successful features of his language around a suitable theme, to display those abrupt expressions and rapid metaphors that break the chains of the present moment, and to make the velocity of his images the very subject matter of his book. And seen that way, everything is simple: We have merely to yield to the temptation and the good fortune of being entertained. But it is possible that the author has sought to do more, vowing to provide an illustration of our era through a study of character and an allegorical tale, attempting to convey to us what monster brought us into the world, and describing the deep-seated nightmare that each of us thinks he finds in the times in which he lives.

Entering this novel whose subject is revealed by its very first words, we find an immediate cause for concern in the sort of digest of himself that Paul Morand appears to have complacently set out there. *The Man in a Hurry* suggests that he accepts the conventional image that people usually have of him. As the novelist of speed, the hero of the tearing hurry, the chronicler of world records, he courts the most vulgar definitions and the crudest epithets, as though taking a certain pleasure in conforming to his legend at a moment when obscurity has begun to make it appear less fatuous. Did he wish to leave a testament that would ironically prove the superficial observer right? Has he tried to recognize himself in the image reflected back at him by a mirror? Has he taken his own playacting seriously? A writer who reveals himself is always trying to achieve some effect, so that the urge to be truthful betrays him just as much as the desire to deceive.

If it were a character study, *The Man in a Hurry* would struggle to construct a figure whose features corresponded to any credible events. What is one to make of this character who says everything there is to be said about himself when he declares melancholically, "I am condemned by fate to gallop full tilt through a universe that merely jogs along"? And the fact is, Pierre Niox cannot stay still; he has to go faster than other people and faster than himself; he is constantly dragged away from the moment he has just alighted at; he goes from walking to driving a car, then from a car to a plane, and from giddy spin to lightning burst without finding a rhythm that can pacify him. It is his fate to yield to a haste for which he sacrifices everything, even time, and to have no other goal than that haste, and this destiny is consumed by the vital forces it requires and then merely expends in the form of a vain and lamentable fever. We are given hundreds of images of this man in a hurry. No sooner has he woken up than he is already far away; his life is organized in such a way that he should never experience any delay; he dresses in a matter of seconds; he eats on the hoof; he barges into performances and causes a disruption; he cuts across conversations. As both an antiquary and an archaeologist, he rides roughshod over the detailed studies he ought normally to carry out, and a lightning voracity drives him this way and that, in a welter of thoughts and actions that threaten him with death at every moment.

Thus nothing could be clearer than this character: He is the man in a hurry, and around him the world reels. But at the same time, if we try to get a firmer grip on him he remains hazy and inconsistent. Possessed as he is by such a demon, it would be easy to accept it if he broke the bounds of verisimilitude and found himself propelled by a monstrous and enigmatic story into a universe for which he alone provided the bizarre measure. In that case, he would require no other justification than his own frenzy. He would carry off as if it were a secret the force that would reunite him at light-speed with the centaurs and the angels. He would exist the way the imaginary does: as an original and absurd creation, launched as a challenge to banal existence, like Lautréamont's hero for example, who is precisely, in his own way, an incarnation of the spirit of aggression and haste. But there is no calculated exaggeration in Morand's book. What he offers us is a life that corresponds to every other life. What is natural is in no way disturbed. The consequences of his furious activity remain modest. There is only a modicum of disorder in the life of the man in a hurry, who often keeps his passion under control and only yields to his follies in his own mind. We are thus almost fatally led to try and understand him in terms of his psychological traits, as a being whose primary characteristic must bring about curious transformations in his mind and in his heart.

But if we resign ourselves to this point of view, we must admit to fresh disappointments. Pierre Niox is only original through the appetite for speed that he possesses, and this life lived at the double leaves him entirely to himself. This tendency does not allow him any inner development. It transforms neither his thoughts not his instincts. He lives by bizarrely linking a perfectly ordinary man with a darting demon, an unbridled, loudmouthed monster who gorges on any number of myths without affecting the mind it is preying upon. Strictly speaking there is no way of understanding him. It is possible at a pinch to conceive of and accept a nightmare being with no links to the real world. But it is impossible to tolerate the invention of a man in whom what is singular in the extreme is unjustifiably adapted to a perfectly banal structure.

There remains the possibility that *The Man in a Hurry* is an allegory, designed through what is natural about it to express each one of us, and to cast light on our civilization through its frightening forms. What is this hero who is so lacking in coherence? A man who, at every moment, is banished from the present by an obscure flame into an insatiable search for the future; a man who seeks with the multiple blows he delivers to forge a frenzied path through time, and who is more attached to being ahead than to being. "I am," he says amusingly, "the man who will be." But this concern for the future gives him no real purchase on time. His impatience and anxiety are expressed through a ravenous obsession, which distances him from the passing moment without bringing him closer to the moment to come. He is merely the most superficial of men, whose mobile soul shows contempt for everything and who, incapable of a single profound perspective on the world, streaks through the night like a meteor without seeing or feeling a thing. Is that the image of our times? Paul Morand finally launches his hero into the fast-moving life of New York, and having experienced the speed of the traffic, the feverish activity, the bounding pace of life, he soon feels the passivity and apathy that are concealed behind all this glittering rush. "No one has ever managed," he says, "to give Americans a sense of the tragic side of life, I mean a sense of its brevity." And this leads him to reflect, as he flies over the immense city at a speed that seems like immobility: "You go fast only on the ground. As soon as I step back and look down at my old planet, it appears to me dead. Speed is a word invented by the earthworm."

Citing such dismal banalities is not a reason for disparaging Paul Morand, since they are inherent in all allegory. All that could be said to him in rejection of this image of our times, namely that the man in a hurry intrinsically belongs to no particular era, that our civilization is no more characterized by feverish haste and the miserable pangs of an unparalleled hunger than Trajan's Rome or Alexandria under the Ptolemies, or that men have always run helter-skelter back and forth between reality and nightmare, nightmare and reality, terrified like animals trapped in a pit, all these generalities designed to show that people do not change would simply provide more clichés, and be as far removed from the truth of our tragedy as is the fable of the man in a hurry. It would in fact be unfair to make a novel responsible for the weak and artificial light that illuminates it, were it not that it appears to rely itself on this mediocre light in order to hold up a mirror for the reader to see and understand himself.

It therefore would seem that we betray Morand's novel far less if we reject any illusion of depth and seek from it a perfectly pleasant story, illustrated by the purest verbal talent. There have been many attempts to explain the movement and originality of this form, which stimulates the mind by subjecting it to all kinds of incantation. Like many writers, like all writers perhaps, Paul Morand makes metaphor the soul of invention. But instead of blending it with what is personal in his style, instead of pursuing it by seeking out the principle of its development, he obliges it to exist entirely within a few words, and allows it to expand by attaching it, with no order and at a very rapid pace, to every moment of the story. The images die as soon as they are created. They momentarily light up certain voices in the sentence then vanish, dispelled by the very light that they cast. They allow neither expectation nor regret. They are like a spring that is constantly compressed and constantly released, that carries all time within itself and consumes it there and then. They are created, destroyed and reconstituted, and are perfect only if they disappear promptly enough for the eye not to be drawn to their excessive color, their fragile form, or the improbable nature of what they mean.

In that respect there are few writers less like Paul Morand than Jean Giraudoux, with whom he is regularly compared. For Giraudoux, metaphor begins by bringing together two things in a seemingly arbitrary fashion, then it develops slowly and solemnly, deriving from this arbitrariness consequences that appear strangely justified, extending its dominion through a dialectic that, with unwavering necessity, pursues its double movement of absurdity and verisimilitude in tandem, before finally, having racked the mind with ever-increasing anguish, culminating in an ultimate image in which paradox and self-evidence match each other with unbearable perfection. For Paul Morand, on the contrary, metaphor, which is devoid of any tragic character, is contained within an immediate figure whose strangeness is justified only by the speed of the gaze that turns toward it and submits to its charm without having time to discover its extravagance. That gives rise to a form in which, thunderstruck rather than enlightened, blind the better to see, the reader perceives golden rocks, dazzling suns, and enchanted lakes that vanish before they can reveal those fogs and broken rays of light that form the reality of every phantasmagoria.

—December 9, 1941

The Sorbonne Novel

The reasons for liking Georges Magnane's *Top of His Class* seem reasonably clear.[1] This long novel about the students of the Latin Quarter is handled with convincing skill. It contains characters, events, and a tissue of factual detail; its composition reflects an image of society, and it is guided by an intention that discreetly transforms the facts it contains. Some will say, "Here is a lifelike novel." Others, suspecting that this Sorbonne novel is inspired by a polemical intention, will ask what is accurate about its view of things. Like many fictions that are linked to a specific historical world, *Top of His Class* will please some people both because it seems to be based entirely on observation, and because in it, observation gives rise to a judgment that transcends or distorts it.

There is no story to speak of in this novel. Georges Magnane has focused on the fates of several students who are working for the *agrégation*. When the examination is over, the novel has finished; and even the events that continue to disrupt the lives of one or two individuals are there merely as a conclusion that sheds light on the true outcome. The subject around which the work is constructed is the disarray that affects young minds that are burdened with the worry caused by a highly competitive examination. The book contains all the elements of a severe judgment on those young intellectuals who willingly destroy themselves with the sole aim of obtaining a qualification, and on the examinations themselves, those immense generators of vacuity into which young heroes of the mind disappear and cease to think about anything. These are the two sides to the drama. Sometimes Magnane shows us young people who are narrow-minded, mediocre, happy with the absurd life they lead and incapable of recognizing its inadequacy. At other times, he is drawn to the fate of more powerful personalities who are vainly attempting to preserve what they are, and whose acts, even when significant, eventually lose all importance.

However, this is not where the interest of the novel would appear to lie, nor where Magnane has sought to locate it. It would not only be a mistake to search for the soul of this book in a thesis that its author has secretly illustrated, but it also would be equally wrong to lend it a sort of mythic significance, such as might be discernible in the distorted, near-fabulous images of a world seen through the eyes of a demonic observer. Georges Magnane did not wish to prove anything by writing his novel, nor did he intend to conjure up a universe full of strange rules, surprising prospects and incomprehensible conventions. Or more precisely, he thought that he would succeed in expressing this universe by creating and giving life to a few people who would reveal what has become of them there.

We may imagine that Magnane came up against a number of obstacles as he pursued this task, and envisage some of the ways in which he sought to overcome them. The first difficulty—it goes without saying that we are not claiming to reconstruct the actual work carried out by the author; that would be absurd; but we are seeking what work he invites the reader to assume he carried out—his first difficulty was that, wishing to portray the dull and humdrum life of the Latin Quarter and having decided, in response to his technical concerns, to present that life through his characters, he was faced with the following alternative: either imagine powerful, typical figures capable of imposing their presence, and in that case encounter the paradox of having to express the dull nonexistence of a world through strong real types; or divide his attention between scarcely visible shadows and run the risk of swamping his novel with the unreality of its subject.

Magnane would seem to have resorted to a number of solutions. He has filled his novel with inconsistent beings whom he calls "minuscules," whose insignificance makes them unnoticeable, and who are so colorless that they exist merely as a sketch for what they could be. They come and go, back and forth: we hardly know they are there. But at the same time, he has created several strong and significant characters, whose originality conveys something quite different from the mediocrity of a superficial milieu, and who robustly bear the weight of the fiction. One of them for example, Gourgaud, a peasant from the Creuse who is hideously ugly and a fiercely solitary worker, is a fundamentally secretive being. A murky episode during a stay in England pursues him like an enigmatic shadow. He is even obliged to flee the Latin Quarter for a while, but he eventually overcomes the fruitless plots that are hatched against him thanks to his rugged good sense. Another character, Carassan, is a subtle creature and is desperately in search of himself. Sorbonne circles mean very little to him. He despises them and spends hardly any time there. He needs adventures that are more real, and capable of giving life meaning. He becomes a volunteer in the Spanish Civil War and is mortally wounded for a cause in which he does not believe.

In certain respects, the paradox of *Top of His Class* clearly lies in the way it convinces us of a certain intellectual banality by portraying people who are exceptional both as individuals and for their history, and in the way it recounts the novel of the Sorbonne by making its protagonists people who fundamentally do not belong to it. One can even argue that the contrast between these exceptional beings and the mediocre society they are meant to reflect would have completely distorted the work, had not Magnane very skillfully managed to fragment these various destinies, alternately illuminating them and casting a shadow over them, varying the light at every moment, capturing them, losing sight of them and then finding them again without ever breaking the thread of their behavior, but also without allowing the superior quality of their natures ever to overwhelm the wretched life they are meant to illustrate. Magnane has the knack of cutting time short, skipping things and inscribing continuity by breaking it, which is the predominant feature of his book. He blends what is essential with what is insignificant, trivial detail with important anecdote thanks to his uncommonly swift resolve. He skillfully imitates chance by varying his perspective on the necessary succession of the facts.

Magnane's other technical concern is to give his characters the greatest possible objectivity. He visibly wants to let them live, as the familiar expression rather opaquely has it: he tries not to intervene in their lives, he refrains from explaining them from without and he does not replace what they appear to be with an analysis of what they are. Magnane applies himself to this endeavor as best he can. Just as his severe verdict on the Sorbonne must not appear as a judgment from without but be deducible from what the characters themselves are, so he endeavors not to make these characters dependent on an extraneous plan or an auxiliary explanation, but rather abandons them to their own life force. The peasant from the Creuse for whom friendship proves a painful ordeal, and who is overwhelmed by examinations, has his own perception of the Sorbonne, just as for Carassan, the desperate indifference with which he resists both affairs of the heart and the cut and thrust of intelligence and politics is peculiar to him. And similarly, every one of the characters, whether episodic or more enduring, forms his or her own view of this world in its remoteness from life and its devotion to words. The reader is not shown the dismal comedy of the Latin Quarter in a single image, simple and complete, which is deployed by the author above the characters' heads, but through a myriad fragmentary images, reflected in mirrors that are sometimes broken, sometimes distorting, and whose rapid succession is designed to create the illusion of a single accurate perspective.

Such was no doubt one of Magnane's ambitions. If he has been unable to fulfill it entirely, it is because he appears to have an inadequate conception of what objectivity means in the novel. If a character in a novel must appear independent of the author, and be the manifestation of an enigma whose key is in no one's hands, as a consequence he is an inaccessible being who reveals himself through a few actions, and about whom things can be said only indirectly. The novel does not only create an individual whom it expresses in his entirety; by indicating what he thinks, says and does, it creates a veritable world all around him, which changes mysteriously with him and, through constant and complete transformations, reflects the reality to which he is linked. We know him only from without. For both author and reader, he is *the other*. In order to prove that their characters have a life of their own, novelists often say: "I am constantly inside my heroes, I identify with them." It is precisely the opposite that they should be proposing: to create characters who are beings with which they can in no way identify, either through imagination, experience, or sensibility.

Georges Magnane identifies too easily with the countless figures he portrays in his book. All the ambiguous relations that can drain them of substance or render them illusory are to be found between him and them. He does not see that the way he approaches them, translates their reactions, and summarizes their thoughts has deadly consequences for genuine objectivity. And in the swirl of detail with which he happily surrounds himself, he gives the impression of perpetuating the unfortunate habits of Naturalism, whereas his primary concern is undoubtedly to steer clear of them. Similarly, he is unable to rid himself of a number of ambiguities that sow confusion in his novel of the Sorbonne. Sometimes the Latin Quarter he describes and that is a reflection of his heroes seems merely to provide a frame for imaginary lives, and precisely to have no other reality than that of an invented world. At others, it appears as an image of the real Latin Quarter, and leaves behind the unpleasant memory of a dismal intellectual sham. What then can be said about these harsh judgments on weak-minded students, absurd examinations, and the entire machine for enfeebling or crushing minds? One is surprised that, on discovering mediocrity, stupidity, and self-satisfaction among young intellectuals, Magnane should consider it grounds for astonishment and a subject of scandal. Whatever did he expect?

—December 16, 1941

Paradoxes on the Novel

Here we have a little book on the novel, accompanied by two novels by young novelists. Chance alone has brought these three books together. The novels may have similar subjects (both are novels about a conversion), but their form, their character, and their significance make them as different from each other as two works can be. They are not opposites, but rather so unlike each other that one does not even notice their differences, and the feeling that they contrast with each other does not help to link them in one's mind. And yet they are both novels, and their common relation to the genre is reinforced by the choice of the themes contained in both of them, and that are generally not to be found in works of fiction. How can this air of strangeness be explained? Is it due to the impurity of the art of the novel? Or is it a sign that this art can be grasped only in the most vague and superficial terms? Kléber Haedens, who has just published a critical essay on the subject, *Paradoxes on the Novel*, will perhaps provide us with a way of seeking an answer.[1]

His book is full of contrasts, seeming contradiction, and bursts of anger, and it constitutes a sly defense of liberty. Novelists, he says, are free to do anything. But what does it mean to "do anything"? As we shall see, not much. Like every legislator who passes laws that abolish every law, Kléber Haedens draws the novelist into a network of ironic concessions and fierce forbearance, the upshot of which is that he is only granted the freedom to do anything so that he can be instructed to do something different from what he has been doing up to now. He is free to submit to other laws.

It is clear from the very first pages of his essay that Kléber Haedens wishes to lure novelists away from fixed rules and make them hate routine. A sensible goal. It is gratifying to hear boldness being praised rather than cozy habit. But the point is: what is routine? Does it consist in obeying a generally accepted rule that you accept without ever having experienced its internal coherence? But you can slavishly obey conventions that only apply to you. And as soon as you follow a rule, even one as common as the three unities, it is perhaps because you consider it necessary, because you have rediscovered it deep inside your mind or intensely and passionately made it your own. Does routine then amount to respect for a bad rule? That would mean that there are good rules. Does it involve consenting unconditionally to an excessively strict and precise convention that will transform a genre capable of infinite diversity into an orderly, monotonous one? Not at all; on the contrary, what Kléber Haedens objects to is the disorder that rules cause: everything is confusion, subjective tyranny and bizarre decree; everyone talks about the true novel, and the true novel remains elusive. Classifications are merely a reflection of anarchy.

Amid this labyrinth of opposing paths, where can Kléber Haedens be heading? Nothing could be clearer. For the fact is, if he is hostile to rules it is to those rules he rejects; and if he thinks critics who talk of the true novel are ridiculous, it is because the definition they have in mind is decidedly inauthentic. What sort of work is a novel for most critics and readers? An imaginary story that, by means of its plot, depicts events that are similar to those in real life or presents characters who could be drawn from everyday existence. And indeed this definition is something we implicitly accept. We have no difficulty in calling the books that correspond to it novels, and we consider those that lie outside it as exceptions, which we admire as if they were wandering stars in a sky into which they were not invited. And yet, says Kléber Haedens most judiciously, none of these characteristics is an essential part of the novel genre. The story? There are extraordinary works, such as Virginia Woolf's *The Waves*, in which plot is not only of no importance, it is imperceptible. The representation of reality? *Suzanne and the Pacific* by Jean Giraudoux, or *Hesperus* by Jean Paul, are novels in which everything is fiction, a rejection of life, and even as trompe-l'oeil they are opposed to tangible reality. Characters who must be created and made lifelike? An absurdity: what about Villier's *Axel* or Achim von Arnim's *Tales*? In Kafka's *Metamorphosis* a traveling salesman wakes up one morning to find he is a beetle; is he a character from real life? In fact, novelists have no reason to think that a novel is good just because the plot is well handled or the heroes come from the normal world. On the contrary, a novelist must beware of the easy options provided by imitation, as well as the false resources of character analysis, psychology, or social history. It is within himself, in his inner dream, that he can best reach the mysterious reality whose revelation can only take place in a novel.

All of the observations that Kléber Haedens makes will provide food for thought to those who like to think about the enigma of the novel as a work of art. But what is more remarkable than those observations themselves is the unease that gives rise to them, and of which they are the profound expression. It turns out that Kléber Haedens is at war with the notion of a rule, rejecting false versions of it and searching for its true forms. He feels that the contemporary novel is unaware of its true chains and is a prisoner of false constraints. Why false ones? He does not say, and it is indeed quite hard to say. It can at least be observed in passing that most of the traditional rules that he denounces tend to offer the novelist, in his struggle against chance, a conventional imitation of chance. To provide a picture of customs, people, and events that reflects their common truth to life is to escape one sort of arbitrariness only to enter a collective one. To write, "The duchess went out at five and had tea with the countess," is to organize one's work by making the observation of a random series of events into its law. The novel requires deeper justifications, and it requires them all the more so because, as Kléber Haedens says, novelists are free to do anything they wish. Since it can be anything, the novel is not justified in being one thing rather than another unless it is that thing completely, not only as a whole but in all of its parts, so that in a novel there should not be a single invented element, a single sentence along with its form, that is not required and rendered necessary by its relation to the whole.

Naturally, such an ideal is not even pursued as something impossible by the art of the novel. Kléber Haedens frequently talks of imperious demands, profound necessities, or visions that the author should espouse entirely. He is not to blame for the vagueness of these expressions; rather, we should conclude from them that for him, the novel's role is to call its author into question to a fearsome degree, to give expression to a universe whose axis is identical to that of his innermost life, in short to give reality to the meaning that a writer gives to his life by creating a world. There is then strictly speaking no longer any such thing as chance. Everything is linked to an inexpressible intention that transfigures the most insignificant events and renders them necessary, so that around them what is random and also what is banal gravitate in a movement that justifies it as banal or random. One should not say that in a work everything should have meaning: it is the work as a whole that should have meaning, and it is perfectly possible that this higher meaning will make one of its conditions a lack of precise meaning or a total absence of intelligibility in some of its parts. There is a type of purity for which the impurity of the alloy is a prerequisite.

What can best reveal the validity of a novel, and show how faithful it is not to the novel genre, but to itself considered as representing on its own the entire genre of the novel, is thus a particular orientation, a mysterious magnetization, the rotation of all the elements of the work around an invisible and constantly mobile center. In order to be able to understand and perhaps judge a book, it is not enough to ask what did its author want to do? Does his book correspond to what he wanted? One should rather ask, what did the book want? Did it want it completely? Where is it headed in that secret state of supreme tension that is its true soul and its primary reason for existing? It is true that questions such as these are misplaced when asked of those many works that entirely lack an inner reality. These novels merely have a subject, and are deprived of those intimate relations with themselves, of that interiority which provides their nocturnal existence. All that can be done is to pass judgment on the interest of that subject, or on the technical perfection that its development displays, both of which are totally inadequate qualities for turning a book into a work equipped with its own necessity. Others resist our curiosity by means of certain tendencies and values whose discretion creates, alongside the real book, a project for a book that provides an object for judgment. In Jacques Perrin's novel *Thy Will Be Done*, the action may appear either absurd or meaningful, depending on our angle of vision.[2] From the standpoint of everyday verisimilitude, which is precisely the one the author adopts, it is hard not to be critical of this brief story of a Communist who, during a passionate affair with a young woman from the internationalist Bolshevik party, realizes that God is watching him, that he is in God's presence. Such a surprising discovery astonishes the young Marxist as much as it does the reader, and indeed strikes him as more unpleasant than disturbing. Without giving it much thought, he continues with his double life as an exemplary atheist, an ardent lover, and a man beheld by God, until one day he is obliged, physically obliged, to undergo a complete conversion. It is clear that if Jacques Perrin had attempted to give his story psychological significance, this would inevitably have led to banality and absurdity. But what makes the novel interesting comes from the unvarying realistic light with which the lovers' tiffs, the bloody political intriguing, and the moments of mysticism are illuminated. Everything happens at the same level of dismal, sordid reality. The sense of the divine is treated just like any other sentiment, its sole originality being its unusual, inexplicable character. It appears in the midst of unbridled orgies, and the budding believer tries vainly to be rid of it using a series of mechanical means. The result is a veritable struggle between opposing influences. God eventually wins, like a champion boxer. Far from betraying the extraordinary experience it is meant to express, this paradoxical realism brings out its incommensurable, inhuman side. But unfortunately, it does not govern the entire book; it is not the "intention" that underlies and composes the episodes; it is there merely as one ingredient, alongside numerous explanations and commentaries. The novel neglects or stifles what gives it its soul.

By contrast, Marius Grout's book *Advent Music* corresponds more consciously to the image that its author has sought to give of it.[3] The subject is a substantial one: A man who is already old believes that he has been given a mission to restore a sense of the miraculous to his village. He is neither a visionary nor is he deranged. He simply believes that if, by means of one or two well-planned actions, he can awaken in his fellow citizens the hope that something marvelous might happen, he will show them the way toward true faith. But he fails. His failure plunges him into a state of extreme spiritual dejection; it seems to him as if God himself has withdrawn from his life. He goes blind. And it is then, in this new night and in the depths of a solitude that he humbly accepts, and having acknowledged the pride and folly of his initial attempt, that he becomes a special being in the eyes of the village, capable of miracles or at least of exemplary actions. With a subject such as this, Marius Grout could have produced a highly ambitious book. That is visibly something he has denied himself. He has reduced the mystery whose darkness he invokes to an abstract transparency. One has the feeling that after devoting a vast, opaque book to his project, he gradually erased it, jettisoning its useless riches and preferring to limit his book to being no more than a project rather than see it vanish beneath obscure and fruitless inventions. Such is the merit of *Advent Music*; such is its secret "intention." Marius Grout has perhaps sacrificed his book to the subtleties of his art, but he has set an example of mastery and attentiveness that, in the domain of the mind, is just as important as a successful book.

—December 30, 1941

Notes

INTRODUCTION

1. Maurice Blanchot, letter to Roger Laporte dated December 22, 1984, in Jean-Luc Nancy, *Maurice Blanchot. Passion politique* (Paris: Galilée, 2011), 59.

2. "Après le désastre," *Journal des Débats*, July 7, 1940, 1. This text reflects the very great tension between what it calls "wounded sentiment," which encourages the mind to withdraw into contemplation, and the urgent need for clear thinking, which must override such soul-searching.

3. Nancy, *Maurice Blanchot*, 59–61.

4. Maurice Blanchot, *Faux pas* (Paris: Gallimard, 1943); *Faux pas*, trans. Charlotte Mandell (Stanford, Calif.: Stanford University Press, 2001). Henceforth *FP*.

5. Nancy, *Maurice Blanchot*, 61.

6. Ibid.

7. "L'ébauche d'un roman," *Aux Écoutes*, July 30, 1938, 31; "The Beginnings of a Novel," trans. Michael Holland, in *The Blanchot Reader*, ed. Michael Holland (Oxford: Blackwell, 1995), 33–34.

8. "Un essai sur Gérard de Nerval," *Journal des Débats*, June 22, 1939, 2; "Une anthologie de la poésie française," *Journal des Débats*, July 20, 1939, 2.

9. "Lautréamont," *Revue Française des Idées et des Œuvres*, no. 1, April 1940, 67–72; *FP*, 172–76.

10. Maurice Blanchot, *Thomas l'obscur* (Paris: Gallimard, 1941); *Thomas the Obscure*, trans. Robert Lamberton (New York: David Lewis, 1973; this is a translation of the new and much shorter version of the novel that appeared in 1950). On April 23, 1940, Blanchot had written to Paulhan about *Thomas*, describing it as "a novel which was completed some time ago," and on May 27 he went into further detail: "it served to help me personally to make progress where there is no longer a path, to move away from the world of psychology and analysis and understand that sentiments and lives can only be experienced profoundly in a place where, as the Upanishads put it, there is neither water, nor light, nor air, nor infinity of space nor infinity of reason, nor total absence of everything nor this world here nor another"; cited by Bernard Baillaud in his preface to Jean Paulhan, *Oeuvres complètes III. Les fleurs de Tarbes* (Paris: Gallimard, 2011), 22.

11. A single number of the journal, dated June 7, 1940, appeared under Maulnier's editorship. This was denounced subsequently, once the usual team was back in control, as a "villainous operation" [*entreprise scélérate*] (see Pierre-Marie Dioudonnat, *Je suis partout 1930–1944. Les Maurrassiens devant la tentation fasciste* (Paris: La Table Ronde, 1973), 327 n. 156). It is noteworthy that on June 8 1940, *Aux Écoutes* hailed the arrest of some of the editors of *Je suis partout*, a journal whose "nefarious activities" had long been denounced by Paul Lévy's weekly.

12. R. [no doubt Lucien Rebatet], "Maurice Blanchot: *Thomas l'obscur* (Gallimard)," *Je suis partout*, October 18, 1941, 8.

13. The manifesto of the movement declares that "the artist can best serve and enlighten the community by creating a work of art," and that to encourage this, "Jeune France will keep its distance from day-to-day events and concentrate on preparing the distant future." See *Jeune France. Principes. Direction. Esprit* (Paris: Editions Jeune France, 1941), 1–2.

14. Quite a detailed account is to be found in Laurence Bertrand Dorléac, *The Art of The Defeat* (Los Angeles: Getty Research Institute, 2008). See in particular chapter 6, "France," 232–75.

15. Maurice Blanchot, "For Friendship," in *Political Writings 1953–1993*, trans. Zakir Paul (New York: Fordham University Press, 2010), 135.

16. Jean Vilar, letter to Andrée Schlegel, in *Cahiers Jean Vilar*, no. 112, March 2012. See also Espace Maurice Blanchot, www.blanchot.fr.

17. See "The Search for Tradition," this volume, for a brief reference to Ambrière, who at the time was a prisoner of war.

18. A copy of this typewritten letter with a note to Raymond Queneau written on it formed part of the Gallimard centenary exhibition at the IMEC in Caen in the autumn of 2009. Included, too, was the list of Gallimard authors that Queneau drew up in response. For the catalogue of the exhibition, see *En toutes lettres: Cent ans de littérature à la Nouvelle Revue française*, ed. Marie-Noëlle Ampoulié, Alban Cerisier, and Eric Legendre (Paris: Gallimard, 2009). Neither Blanchot's letter nor Queneau's list is included in the catalogue, but they can be viewed at www.centenaire-nrf.fr/entouteslettres/cimaise5.swf. The criterion for selecting these "representative" authors was that they should display both rigor and a willingness to make a radical break (*une double volonté de rupture et de rigueur*).

19. Jean Lacouture, *Paul Flamand, éditeur* (Paris: Éditions des Arenes, 2010), 51. Paul Flamand, who founded the Éditions du Seuil, was one of the founders of Jeune France, along with Pierre Schaeffer.

20. See "For Friendship," 135: "Paul Flamand also found our conception of culture too 'lofty.'" In *Les antennes de Jericho* (Paris: Stock, 1978), Pierre Schaeffer recalls that Blanchot and Lignac were "ruthless critics of my ideas, intransigent defenders of the integrity of the artist" (278).

21. See "For Friendship," 136. His remark on collaboration is in a letter to Jeffrey Mehlman dated November 26, 1979, in Jeffrey Mehlman, *Legacies of Anti-Semitism in France* (Minneapolis: University of Minnesota Press, 1983), 146.

22. Maurice Blanchot, *Chroniques littéraires du* Journal des Débats. *Avril 1941–août 1944* (Paris: Gallimard, 2007). Bident offers an illuminating account of the way Blanchot's cultural ventures are reflected in the chronicles that he publishes in 1941 and 1942. See Christophe Bident, *Partenaire invisible* (Seyssel: Champ Vallon, 1998), 218–23.

23. See, for example, the reference to the "various projects being pursued by young men" in "The Writers' Silence."

24. See "La France, nation à venir," *Combat*, no. 19, (November 1937), 131–32.

25. See "The Search for Tradition."

26. Raymond Dumay's descriptions of a rural idyll in the Saône-et-Loire, the *départment* where Blanchot was born, elicit a seemingly nostalgic response that is rather moving.

27. In 1942 Blanchot will refer to "the cross-fire between Paul Valéry and the Surrealists." See "Lamartine's Position," *FP*, 153.

CHRONICLE OF INTELLECTUAL LIFE I

1. This was the first of Blanchot's chronicles to appear in the *Journal des Débats*. It was without a title.

2. Jean de Baroncelli, *Vingt-six hommes* (Paris: Grasset, 1941).

3. Jacques Benoist-Méchin, *La moisson de 40* (Paris: Albin Michel, 1941); Maurice Betz, *Dialogues de prisonniers 1940* (Paris: Émile-Paul, 1940).

4. Pierre Mac Orlan, *Chronique de la fin d'un monde* (Paris: Émile-Paul, 1940); Jacques Chardonne, *Chronique privée de l'an 40* (Paris: Stock, Delamain et Boutelleau, 1941).

5. Irène Français, *J'étais une petite fille* (Paris: Denoël, 1941).

6. Raymond Dumay, *L'herbe pousse dans la prairie* (Paris: Gallimard, 1941).

7. Charles-François Landry, *Baragne* (Lausanne: La Guilde du Livre, 1939; Paris: Gallimard, 1941).

8. Henri Mondor, *Vie de Mallarmé I* (Paris: Gallimard, 1941).

9. Marcel Arland, *Anthologie de la poésie française* (Paris: Stock, Delamain et Boutelleau, 1941); Thierry Maulnier, *Introduction à la poésie française* (Paris: Gallimard, 1939).

10. Montesquieu, *Cahiers 1716–1755* (Paris: Grasset, 1941).

11. Daniel Halévy, *Péguy et Les Cahiers de la Quinzaine* (Paris: Grasset, 1941); Friedrich Nietzsche, *Naissance de la tragédie*, trans. Geneviève Bianquis (Paris: Gallimard, 1940); Søren Kierkegaard, *Post-scriptum aux miettes philosophiques*, trans. Paul Petit (Paris: Gallimard, 1941).

THE WRITERS' SILENCE

1. Jean Bazaine, "Guerres et évasions," *Nouvelle Revue française* 326 (April 1941), 621–22.

CHRONICLE OF INTELLECTUAL LIFE 2

1. Jean de Baroncelli, *Vingt-six hommes* (Paris: Grasset, 1941).
2. Jacques Benoist-Méchin, *La moisson de 40* (Paris: Albin Michel, 1941)

TWO NOVELS

1. Raymond Dumay, *L'herbe pousse dans la prairie* (Paris: Gallimard, 1941).
2. Charles-François Landry, *Baragne* (Lausanne: La Guilde du Livre, 1939; Paris: Gallimard, 1941).

FRANCE AND CONTEMPORARY CIVILIZATION

1. Lucien Maury, ed., *Définitions de la France: à diverses époques/ par des souverains, hommes d'état, écrivains, artistes français et étrangers* (Paris: Stock, Delamain et Boutelleau, 1941); Paul Valéry et al., *La France et la civilisation contemporaine* (Paris: Flammarion, 1941). There is no separate volume entitled *Études françaises*.
2. Paul Valéry, "La pensée et l'art français," in *La France et la civilisation contemporaine*, 5–18.
3. Paul Valéry, *Réflections sur le monde actuel* (Paris: Stock, Delamain et Boutelleau, 1931); *Reflections on the World Today*, trans. Francis Scarfe (New York: Pantheon Books, 1948; London, Thames & Hudson, 1951).
4. Paul Valéry, "La pensée et l'art français," 18.
5. Richard Wagner, *Souvenirs*, trans. Camille Benoît (Paris: Carpentier, 1884), 284.
6. Joseph de Maistre, *Trois fragments sur la France* (1794), in *Écrits sur la révolution* (Paris: PUF, 1989), 81–85, 88–89.

THE ART OF MONTESQUIEU

1. Montesquieu, *Cahiers 1716–1755*, ed. Bernard Grasset (Paris: Grasset, 1941).
2. Montesquieu, *Pensées et fragments inédits* (Bordeaux: Imprimerie G. Gounouilhou, 1899), 1:104.

THE SEARCH FOR TRADITION

1. Robert Francis, *Souvenirs imaginaires* (Paris: Gallimard, 1941).
2. Jean Vignaud was the president of the Société des Gens de Lettres and a member of Vichy's Conseil National.

THE NOVEL AND POETRY

1. Jacques Audiberti, *Urujac* (Paris: Gallimard, 1941).

CULTURE AND CIVILIZATION

1. Paul Valéry, "The Crisis of the Mind" (1919), in *Paul Valéry: An Anthology*, ed. James R. Lawler (London: RKP, 1977), 102.
2. Pierre-Simon Ballanche, *Le vieillard et le jeune homme*, ed. Roger Mauduit (Paris: Alcan, 1929), 53–96.
3. Lucien Febvre, "*Civilisation*. Évolution d'un mot et d'un groupe d'idées," in *Civilisation. Le mot et l'idée*, ed. Lucien Febvre et al. (Paris: La Renaissance du Livre, 1930), 1–55.
4. Ballanche, *Le vieillard et le jeune homme*, 74.

IN PRAISE OF RHETORIC

1. Maurice Garçon, *L'éloquence judiciaire* (Paris: Mercure de France, 1941). Blanchot's article does not appear in the "Chroniques de la vie intellectuelle" column but on the first page of the *Journal des Débats*, entirely in italics, under the heading "Day by Day" (*Au Jour le Jour*).
2. This sentence is omitted in the Gallimard version.

A VIEW OF DESCARTES

1. "Une vue de Descartes," in *Les Pages immortelles de Descartes, choisies et expliquées par Paul Valéry* (Paris: Éditions Corrêa, 1941), 7–66; "A View of Descartes," in *The Living Thoughts of Descartes, Presented by Paul Valéry*, trans. H. L. Binsse (London: Cassell, 1948), 12–94.

2. Karl Jaspers, *Descartes und die Philosophie* (Leipzig: W. de Gruyter & Co., 1937); *Descartes et la philosophie*, trans. Hans Poll-now (Paris: Librairie Félix Alcan, 1937); in *Leonardo, Descartes, Max Weber: Three Essays*, trans. Ralph Mannheim (London: Routledge & Kegan Paul, 1965).

A NOVEL BY MAURIAC

1. François Mauriac, *La Pharisienne* (Paris: Grasset, 1941); *A Woman of the Pharisees*, trans. Gerard Hopkins (London: Eyre & Spottiswoode, 1946).
2. This is a reference to Alain-René Lesage's novel *Le diable boîteux* (1707), translated as *The Devil Upon Two Sticks*.

YOUNG NOVELISTS

1. Raymond Guérin, *Quand vient la fin* (Paris: Gallimard 1941).
2. Raymond Guérin, *Zobain* (Paris: Gallimard, 1936). Blanchot wrote a review of this novel in *L'Insurgé* 7 (February 17, 1937), 5.
3. Paul Gadenne, *Siloé* (Paris: Gallimard, 1941).

THEATER AND THE PUBLIC

1. Jacques Copeau, *Pour un théâtre populaire* (Paris: PUF, 1941).
2. Pierre-Aimé Touchard, *Dionysos—Apologie pour le théâtre* (Paris: Aubier-Montaigne, 1938), 19. The lines by Claudel are taken from "La maison fermée," in *Cinq grandes odes* (Paris: Éditions de la Nouvelle Revue française, 1913); *Five Great Odes*, trans. Edward Lucie-Smith (London: Rapp & Carroll, 1967). It should be noted that the last word in Blanchot's text, "*sourd*" (deaf), is a misprint and should in fact read "*lourd*."

MEDITERRANEAN INSPIRATIONS

1. Jean Grenier, *Inspirations méditerranéennes* (Paris: Gallimard, 1940).
2. Charles Maurras, *Anthinea. D'Athènes à Florence* (Paris: Flammarion, 1901).

UNKNOWN OR UNDERRATED AUTHORS

1. Valéry Larbaud, *Domaine français* (Paris: Gallimard, 1941).

2. Nicolas Boileau, "7e Réflexion sur Longin," in *Les réflexions sur Longin et pages choisies de toute son œuvre*, edited by M. Bonfantini and S. Zoppi (Turin: Giappichelli, 1965).

3. Paul Valéry, "La jeune parque," in *Œuvres complètes* (Paris: Gallimard, 1959), 1:396; "The Young Fate," in *The Collected Works of Paul Valéry*, ed. Jackson Matthews (New York: Pantheon Books, 1956), 1:94.

4. Philothée O'Neddy, *Feu et flamme* (1833), ed. Marcel Hervier (Paris: Editions des Presses Françaises, 1926).

5. Philothée O'Neddy, "Le cul de jatte," in *Œuvres posthumes* (Paris: G. Charpentier, 1877), 272–84.

6. Maurice Scève, *Microcosme*, with an introduction by Valéry Larbaud (Mastricht: A. A. M. Stols, 1928).

7. Jean de Lingendes, "Ode sur le deuil de la reine," in *Œuvres poétiques*, ed. E. T. Griffiths (Manchester: Manchester University Press, 1916), 17.

TERROR IN LITERATURE

1. Jean Paulhan, *Les fleurs de Tarbes, ou La terreur dans les lettres* (Paris: Gallimard, 1941); *The Flowers of Tarbes, Or, Terror in Literature*, trans. Michael Syrotinski (Champaign: University of Illinois Press, 2006).

2. This is the first of three articles that Blanchot devoted to Jean Paulhan's book *The Flowers of Tarbes*, and the only one not to be included in *Faux pas*. See "How is literature possible?" *FP*, 76–84.

THE WRITER AND THE PUBLIC

1. Jacques-Napoléon Faure-Biguet, *Les enfances de Montherlant* (Paris: Plon, 1941).

2. Henri de Montherlant, *La petite infante de Castille* (Paris: Grasset, 1929); *Aux fontaines du désir*, volume 1 of *Les voyageurs traqués* (Paris: Grasset, 1927); *Service inutile* (Paris: Grasset, 1935);

"La paix dans la guerre," *Nouvelle Revue française* 331 (September 1941), 257–68.

3. "Allocution 15 mai 1934," in *Service inutile*, 16–20.

HUYSMANS'S SECRET

1. Joris-Karl Huysmans, *La cathédrale* (Paris: Stock, 1898); *The Cathedral*, trans. Clara Bell (London: Dedalus, 1989).

2. Lucien Descaves, *Les dernières années de J.-K. Huysmans* (Paris: Albin Michel, 1941); Maurice Garçon, *Huysmans inconnu. Du bal du Château-Rouge au monastère de Ligugé* (Paris: Albin Michel, 1941).

3. Joris-Karl Huysmans, *En route* (Paris: Tresse & Stock, 1895); *En Route*, trans. C. Kegan Paul (London: Kegan Paul, 1896).

THE MAN IN A HURRY

1. Paul Morand, *L'homme pressé* (Paris: Gallimard, 1941).

THE SORBONNE NOVEL

1. Georges Magnane, *La bête à concours* (Paris: Gallimard, 1941).

PARADOXES ON THE NOVEL

1. Kléber Haedens, *Paradoxes sur le roman* (Paris: Editions du Sagittaire, 1941).

2. Jacques Perrin, *Que votre volonté soit faite* (Paris: Gallimard, 1941).

3. Marius Grout, *Musique d'Avent* (Paris: Gallimard, 1941).

Index